You and Me

Travel, Misadventures, and Love Around the World

MICHAEL S. RYAN &
KRISTEN HERRINGTON

 FriesenPress

Suite 300 - 990 Fort St
Victoria, BC, V8V 3K2
Canada

www.friesenpress.com

Copyright © 2021 by Michael S. Ryan & Kristen Herrington
First Edition — 2021

ISBN
978-1-03-910904-9 (Hardcover)
978-1-03-910903-2 (Paperback)
978-1-03-910905-6 (eBook)

1. *Travel*

Distributed to the trade by The Ingram Book Company

Table of Contents

Prologue

There are only so many scenic pictures and "our trip was so awesome" stories you can hear from someone before you want to pour acid down their throats so they never utter another word again. We get it: your trip was amazing and we should all be jealous. But for every perfect picture of drinking a mai tai at sunset on top of a volcano, there's the missed cab, blisters on your feet, waking up to a lizard in your bed, and a sweaty shirt that smells like Sidney Crosby's unwashed lucky underwear at the end of a season.

People don't often tell you about these moments because they want to appear as though they have their shit together. Telling you about the time they *actually* shit themselves would say otherwise. Humans have a tendency to want to appear better than they actually are. Take a look at ANY SOCIAL MEDIA ACCOUNT IN THE WORLD. It's a barrage of curated moments showcasing people at their best, accentuating the good, hiding the bad. This is never more apparent than with travelling.

While we're far from Marco Polo, we've travelled enough to experience the spectrum of ups and downs in the hustle of moving from one place to the next. The good moments certainly do exist, and we tried to capture them too. But the reality is that to get to them a lot of stuff happens along the way. It may not be pretty all the time, but that's the stuff you remember most. And that's the stuff worth repeating.

Our relationship as a couple grew and was tested during these moments. To quote ourselves (it's our book, we can do whatever the hell we want!) from the story, "Koko's Masterpiece: Love and Shit," *There's only so much you can learn about someone when you're dressed up and talking over a candle-lit dinner drinking martinis. You either fall apart or bond and become inseparable when you're sharing a small room and have only eaten curry for a month.*

We'll take you on our journeys throughout Costa Rica, Thailand, Columbia, Europe, America and our tiny hometowns on Canada's east coast. Told through a collection of non-chronological short stories, we reflect on our last decade's worth of adventure together. The backdrop is travel and the story is love—from subways to sunsets, pad thai to "bear ties," this is us warts and all. Yeah . . . mainly the warts.

Michael's stories are in this **FONT**.

Kristen's stories are in this ℱONT.

You'll figure out the rest.

M & K

JUST MARRIED

66What about that guy standing in the water?" Kristen suggested.

"The drug dealer?" I asked.

I guess he did look capable. He had hands and wasn't violently shaking—two of my top three criteria. He had to be a bit of a go-getter too. It was 7 a.m. and he was already in the water trying to move some dope. That was the kind of man I wanted.

I woke at about 6 a.m. Kristen was already up and said we should get married now. I agreed. We hadn't really told anyone other than our parents, close friends, and travel agent (rumour was that we might get a free bottle of champagne if she told the resort). We wanted it to be simple. No senile old relatives inadvertently speaking aloud their mildly racist thoughts about our non-white friends, no drunk uncles challenging people they don't know to arm-wrestles, no barely touched plates of food we paid $50 a head for, and no moms swooning over weird looking babies that actually look like The Predator. The goal was no headaches and no thinking about any decision for more than the length of a Superbowl commercial.

We got showered and cleaned up. Kristen thought about doing her hair fancy, but with the humidity and fact that we'd be half drunk and line dancing poolside in a few hours, she said fuck it. Twenty minutes later, we walked along the beach until we found a tree we both liked. It was a little sideways but had leaves and wasn't rotten so it met our standards.

With the morning waves lightly crashing and the sunrise lighting up the world with a perfect hint of all the right colours, five years to the day we met, we stood under the crooked tree, said our vows and exchanged rings. Our rings were made by a hipster Venezuelan art student with three fingers. We didn't specifically go looking for a cool, three-fingered South American ring maker, but we were glad that's who we found.

Kristen wore a white dress she got at Value Village for $8.99. She had ordered another that didn't come in on time so bought this the day before we left. She wore her ma's pearls, lip gloss and sandals from Old Navy that someone had left at our house and were chewed up by a dog.

I had a white dress shirt, pants I was calling dress pants but that would likely fail dress-code at any bar that sells more than beer and hard liquor, Birkenstocks, and a "bear tie." A bear tie is a tie that depicts scenes of bears doing general bear activities. This was an exceptionally good bear tie.

> **TRAVEL TIP:** *Travel with clothes that you're not attached to. If you spill a bottle of mustard on yourself or forget the T-shirt that you took off to swing above your head when "Groove is in the Heart" came on in a bar, you won't be upset. If it's valuable to you, leave it behind.*

We kissed under the tree and both smiled. Our hearts gushed and the feel-good chemicals in our bodies flowed uncontrollably. We needed to capture the moment. We needed to be able to return to this feeling, this beautiful aliveness any time we wanted.

"We need a picture," Kristen declared with excitement.

I agreed. This was the happiest I'd ever felt. I wanted the moment solidified, a definitive snapshot of who we were and how we felt.

"Who can take it?" I asked.

He had been there the entire time—eyes slightly bugging out of his head, a modest smile somewhere between maniacal and lovable. His skin was oily, and not in the good "I'm lubed up and working on my sweet tan" kind of way. He was greasy because he was a greasy human—sickly thin, probably owned at least two Insane Clown Posse albums, and it appeared as though a colony of birds were nesting in his matted hair, preparing intently for a change of seasons that never comes.

"I'll go talk to him," I told Kristen.

I don't know the exact legalities of selling drugs at resorts in Jamaica, but it appears that if you're ankle deep in water, all is good. I walked towards him, a man who undoubtedly had the "good stuff" and would soon be offering it to me. Half way towards him I turned back and looked at my wife for the first time. Her blonde hair waved in the slight breeze. The sun bounced off her shiny white dress and she glowed like the sum of all my best dreams put together. "I'm a lucky fucking man," I thought to myself.

There was a little back and forth about drugs, pills and whatnot, but in the end, he seemed flattered. He stepped out of the water and came towards us. Kristen gave him her phone and he snapped away. The pictures turned out about exactly the way you'd expect if you hired a Jamaican drug dealer to be your wedding photographer. Sixty per cent had his thumb in them, a few were just closeups of Kristen's breasts, and his concept of framing was akin to a child trying to decipher ancient Egyptian hieroglyphs. But the moment's there. Our faces, the tree, the feeling. That's all that mattered in the end.

We thanked our personal Robert Frank and he went back to the water to try to make some early morning cheddar. He said he'd see us at the pool later, that he was a lifeguard there too. I saluted him and knew that we were in good hands.

Our wedding meal was the breakfast buffet. We loaded up on bacon and had dessert before 9 a.m. because it was our goddamn wedding and we could do what we wanted. We played ping-pong, drank Krazy Koconuts, and swam in the ocean. For our reception we found a band playing on the beach and pretended all the songs were for us. That night we went to a French restaurant and held hands under the stars.

It was the perfect day in every way. For us, anyway.

I knew that a million adventures lay ahead. That our love for travel, our like-mindedness, our shared mentality to do things inexpensively (or be cheap bastards, some friends may say), and desire to do it all our own way would lead to a life we both wanted and needed. It was the start of it all. And I couldn't wait.

LIEUTENANT DAN

When you grow up in a place famous for having the highest tides in the world, you don't often think that tidal bores will be of significance elsewhere. In Nova Scotia, the tides can reach up to 16-metres high—or the height of three giraffes standing on each other's heads. In other words, really fucking high. It's something I took for granted (didn't care about) growing up and, quite honestly, have been scared of the ocean since I was a victim of a shark attack when I was eight and vacationing in Florida with my family. The "shark" was really a dolphin and the "attack" was really just playful bobbing super far away from me. But there WAS a beach full of people waving their hands over their head screaming "SHARK!!!!" and that's enough to scar a person for life when it comes to bodies of water other than puddles and pools.

If Mike and I are travelling in warm places, I'll still "go in" the ocean. My limit is typically to the point where the water covers my kneecaps. To go deeper, my trick is to maintain a constant death grip around Mike's neck to make sure I'm both kept afloat and he can fight off any minnows or strands of leg-brushing-seaweed in my honour. Swimming in the ocean is mostly anxious thrashing that I endure long enough to get my wavy beach hair and then I'm happy to watch from afar for the remaining 10 hours of beach time.

In addition to beach days, there have been plenty of times where we have had to take a ferry or small power boat from place to place. I don't usually mind these rides and am aware that if I do go overboard, I am more likely to die from a heart attack before any creature would have the opportunity to nibble on my elbows or nose and have accepted that's how I would go.

We have been on some questionable boats—usually rusty, leaking oil, or named *Tammy*—but for the most part, captains have been capable, and the crew have been caring.

But there's always an exception to "for the most part." Otherwise, it would be "for the always part" and people don't say that about travelling in foreign countries. "For the most part, you'll be safe, healthy, fed and free from tidal bores," they say. And so, we take that chance that we will be "mostly" safe from being swallowed by the darkness and distress of the ocean demons below that you can't see but have conscious nightmares about.

Until we visited Koh Samet in Thailand, I was an "always part" kind of girl. At least when it came to boats, safety and tidal bores.

Mike and I, and about 40 white-haired Chinese tourists vacationing on the same island that weekend, boarded a rusty, oil-leaking ship named *Phûĥying bā* (which I assumed was the Thai equivalent to Tammy) destined for the mainland just over an hour's ride away. It was a clear sky and hot as hell like every other day in Thailand. At the end of the pier where the boat was docked, there was a giant statue coming out of the water. It was a figure, the size of two giraffes standing on each other's heads, of a scary woman bearing her ungodly large breasts. We're not sure the significance of the statue or why it existed. Maybe it *was* just a woman with huge breasts. Who wouldn't want that massive statue at the departure site of their quaint community? If something were to go down on the water, at least the last thing you'd see before disappearing to the sea forever would be the unfathomably large breasts of a bronzed goddess.

Like typical Canadians, we let everyone else board the boat before us. We had to store our backpacks under a metal seat, covered with hundreds of layers of paint. I wondered how many inches lower the seats were when the boat was brand new? We didn't get a seat of our own but could keep an eye on our packs from the deck of the single-level vessel.

Something else we didn't get were life jackets. There were exactly enough for every other passenger on board other than me and Mike. I watched as the other passengers slipped on their CRUCIAL LIFE-SAVING DEVICES and sat down on their moderately comfortable seats. We stood at the back wearing dirty tank tops and Canadian expressions that meant "don't worry about us." I was, in fact, worried. Mike was completely unfazed. He said that if the boat went down, everyone else on board were senior citizens who looked like they'd lived a full and enjoyable life. If he had to snag a few life jackets off of their tiny sinking bodies for our own survival, it wouldn't be too big a loss.

It was a medium-sized boat—probably two and a half giraffes long— and it was a calm day on the water. We found a place to stand near the bow of the boat and cozied up next to each other for a peaceful journey back to the mainland. Despite the inevitable feast the beach ants had had on Mike's feet, or the electrical plugs in our hotel that were so high on the wall we actually needed a ladder to reach, we had enjoyed our time in Koh Samet. We were relaxed and in the groove of travel bliss. This feeling takes a while to achieve. You need to be in the thick of it. When the days start to roll together, the unfamiliar starts to feel like the norm, and your tan is like cinnamon on toast. We looked out onto the water, arms wrapped around each other and smiled onto the sunny sea life below.

Exactly halfway into the boat ride, equally between one piece of land and another, I noticed the colour of the sky change. It went from a gentle puppy's kiss to a raging witch's brew in a matter of seconds. I tugged on Mike's shirt to draw his attention to the mood-swinging sky.

The black clouds overwhelmed the cotton balls that were there just moments ago and started charging towards us in record speed. I could see the boat crew shifting back and forth, exchanging words and not hiding their concerned expressions. Their anxiety was contagious. It was inevitable that we'd hit the weather head-on. We were in the direct centre of the body of water and couldn't turn back. The only option was to trudge forward, to push on.

Within minutes, the storm was above us, under us and on us. The walls of salty seawater rose and sank in a taunting rhythm. The waves appeared to be threatening us with their girth and power as they raced towards us with confidence. Rain squalls were rocking the boat back and forth like an undecided bowling pin, just struck by the marble ball. The wind was so strong, pieces of debris and fishing nets started whipping past our faces. The sky was midnight and the ocean a churning blender of demise and despair.

I was paralyzed. I was in my most terrifying scenario, with no life-jacket, no English-speaking people, and certainly no skill set to manage my physical or mental well-being under the circumstances. My clothes were completely soaked. I dropped to the deck into the fetal position, staring up at the bobbing ceiling of the many-times-painted boat and praying for the first time in my life. I'm not sure to whom, but would have welcomed anyone from Buddha to Betty White so long as they planned to save me from falling over the edge of the boat that was now spilling over with water.

I looked up at Mike, my eyes filled with fear and tears. While I was curled up like an unborn baby, Mike had become Lieutenant Dan. If you've ever seen this scene in *Forrest Gump*, you'll be familiar with the utter glory that this character expresses during a perfectly comparable storm. With pure joy running through his blood, smile consuming his face and cheering the storm on like it was just about to break an Olympic record, my otherwise mild-mannered husband was in his absolute, epic glory. One hand gripped the railing, the other raised in the air with a clenched fist celebrating the matchless power of the death storm. Equally wet and life-jacketless, Mike had transformed into a madman, ready to defeat the wild weather. Though we have so much in common, this scenario revealed our opposite responses to what I would call nothing less than a crisis. For Mike, this was no more concerning than a burned-out lightbulb or leaky faucet. He was having *fun*!

The tourists were huddled in groups, likely sharing their last wishes and messages to family members with each other in hopes they would be passed on. I crawled on my stomach to our backpacks and dug out our passports. "At least if we die, they'll know who we were," I figured. "At least we had one last adventure together, got to feel the sun on our skin and eat the best pad thai we'd ever had."

Mike was shouting things to me through his laughter and glee. It was too loud and chaotic to decipher his words, but I imagined he was telling me he loved me. That he was grateful to have shared this life with me. That if we were going to die, at least it would be together . . .

After 20 minutes of movie-like terror, the blackness of the clouds softened to a muted grey, the grey to cream, the cream to white. The waves eased and the boat began to find balance again, moving forward instead of side to side. The Chinese tourists loosened their grips from their luggage and each other. I peeled myself up off the deck, soaked in water from the sky, the sea and my eyes. I could see mainland in the distance. I could see safety. I could see Mike's happy face looking over at me with reassurance and confidence.

"See?! That wasn't so bad," he exclaimed.

DRUGS:

Big Guy Like the Weed

No matter where we go in the world I'm offered drugs within 30 minutes of arrival. Something about me screams, "I need drugs immediately! Strangers, please approach!" Drug dealers zero in on me with laser focus. They see me coming from miles away and in their hearts and minds have determined that I—"Big Guy"—need something. It doesn't matter where we are. It doesn't matter if there's a language barrier or not. Every place in the world has the universal sign of "fingers to lips" to represent marijuana or "finger on nostril and snorting" for cocaine.

I'm not against anyone using drugs. Whatever people want to do is fine with me, and also none of my business. Personally, I don't really indulge anymore. I say not really because about every two years I try to smoke a joint in hopes of feeling relaxed, enjoying ice cream a little more, understanding David Lynch movies, etc. It usually ends up just making me paranoid and thinking about snakes, so I hang it up for another 700 days or so until I think it's a good idea again.

In Thailand we decided to go to Koh Phi Phi. It's a place as beautiful as any in the world; a tropical paradise with turquoise water, white sand beaches and stunning rock formations. The movie *The Beach* with Leonardo DiCaprio was shot close by. That's about all we knew about it, and that was enough for us.

We got on a ferry in Phuket and zoomed along with about 200 others. It wasn't long into the ride that I realized I was the only guy on board without a six-pack and capable of starting a sentence without

"DUUUUDE!" Muscular, tanned guys in their early 20s with no shirts on puffed out their chests for the equivalent, skinny female versions in bikinis. I grabbed at the rolls on my sides and thought about sit-ups. In these situations, it's an obligation for human males to suck in their guts. For millions of years, our species has perfected the task of trying to appear less chubby to people who are, in fact, less chubby. Engrained in our DNA is the ability to hide excess fat by body manipulation. I was sucking in so hard I started to exert muscles that anatomy has not yet discovered. My face strained and Kristen thought I was having a heart attack.

We didn't know beforehand, but Phi Phi is a party island. It's where kids just old enough to buy a pack of smokes go to get blackout drunk and make stupid decisions. At 32, we both felt old. We had made the majority of our idiotic choices in life and were more or less there for the coconuts and warm water. In the end, we'd at least get a laugh out of the primal mating rituals and general moronic behaviour of our fellow travellers.

As the boat approached the harbour, the 198 millennials—and us— started to unload. There, waiting on the shore, a small Thai man zeroed in on me. He made eye contact and smiled like I was an old friend.

He pointed directly towards me.

"Is that little fella pointing at me?" I asked Kristen.

"It definitely looks that way," she said as we jumped ashore with our bags.

He smiled and nodded his head repeatedly. None of the other people mattered whatsoever, they were invisible to him. "Big Guy like the weed!" he yelled as he walked towards us.

That's another guarantee. While travelling, it's set in stone that every male I communicate with will refer to me as "Big Guy." Some guiding intuition in the big frequency of the universe will pull the words out of them when they lay eyes upon me.

Like most drug dealers, he was a short, tiny little human, shrivelled up and dried out like a raisin. He made the universal "would you be interested in buying marijuana, sir?" gesture and stood in front of us.

It was strange because there were so many other people around. Piles of 20-year-olds, who CLEARLY wanted someone to sell them drugs, sur-rounded us. They'd soon empty into the town, their minds set decisively on finding mind-altering substances. His target audience was ample and everywhere. But they didn't matter to this man. No one did but me. He was surrounded by a sea of Michael Jordans with a basketball in his hand, but somehow arrived at the oddly shaped—and out of shape—white guy to try and get the ball to.

While drug dealers have universal signs and symbols for their whole-saling, I, as a consumer, have learned the appropriate gestures for my side of the transaction. I gave the thumbs up—the universal sign for "Thanks for the offer, bud, but I'm currently fine. I appreciate you taking the time to approach me, though."

I'm aware that sometimes a straight up "no" would be best. Or to not engage at all. If I just kept walking, if I didn't even look at him. But deep down that doesn't feel right. I can't not look in his direction just because he makes his living selling illegal substances to tourists. He probably watches *Golden Girls* reruns like the rest of us and tells someone he loves them before bed every night.

"I see you around," he said slowly and smiling the whole time. I gave the thumbs up again and kept walking, the drones of kids around us pushing on to find the party.

That night there was fire dancing across the whole beach. "Wow," I said, marvelling at our luck. "We must have arrived on some special occasion!" Music blasted and people across the beach twisted and twirled with things on fire—skipping ropes, hula hoops, things they juggle, and so on. I didn't know it at the time, but if you walk down any beach anywhere in Thailand at night and there's *not* fire dancing, the apocalypse has likely arrived.

A strange thing began to happen on Koh Phi Phi. Everywhere I went I'd see the little drug dealer man. Bobby. That's what I decided to call him. Bobby seemed to always know I was coming. He'd be there smiling like he was waiting for me, like it was a predetermined meeting point and I arrived exactly on time. The first night, in a crowd of a hundred or so people, I saw little Bobby across from me, his smiling face lit up from the fire and appearing even shorter than earlier that day. In the town at restaurants, at night in bars. It didn't matter. He was there. I remember walking through the woods with Kristen, holding hands and looking for a secluded place to smooch. Bobby popped up from behind a tree. In the fucking woods! "Big Guy!" he called out, nodding and flashing his yellow drug dealer teeth. If I was actually trying to hide from Bobby, that would have been the place I'd go. It was the most hidden area we could find on the entire island. It was probably the last place we should have been due to the numerous spiders, lizards, and weird creatures that could get us. But somehow, Bobby knew we'd be there.

I soon realized that it was inevitable. I had to buy drugs from Bobby. Kristen would smoke it. I'd surprise her with it and she'd think I was the bravest man in the world. She'd cook me supper every night for eternity and hire the world's greatest statue builder to memorialize my heroic moment in permanent stone. There was also the chance that maybe Bobby was some kind of undercover cop trying to pin me. As soon as I made the purchase, I'd be in cuffs and off to Thai prison for life. I thought about the gangs that would be in there and who I'd side with. I'd try to find a nice group of friends who liked hockey and '90s grunge music. We'd spend our days laughing and making spaghetti together like they did in *Goodfellas*. The only bad thing is that I'd be, by far, the biggest guy in the whole jail. There's that old prison adage that to establish your toughness when you first go in, you find the biggest guy you can and fight him to prove your worth. I'm basically Andre the Giant in Thailand so I'd be done for. All the new prisoners would come for me. The greasy Thai kick-boxer criminals would bust my ribs while I try to explain that I'm a good, down-to-earth Canadian boy who got caught in the wrong place at the wrong time and only wants to make spaghetti and talk about Nirvana with my buds. All because I bought weed from Bobby.

But it was a risk I had to take. If I let it go any longer, Bobby would soon be in our hotel bathroom in the middle of the night when I went to take a leak. "Big Guy!" he'd say as always, smiling. I'd turn the light off and go back to bed, hoping not to find him under the covers.

I wanted to surprise Kristen with the weed. I knew there was a chance I'd go to prison, so I left a note:

> *Out for a walk. If I'm not back in 20 minutes,*
> *I'm likely in prison.*
> *Love you!*
> *Mike xo*

I left while she was still in bed. I knew that all I had to do was walk anywhere and Bobby would be there. I walked into the town, past the pad thai lady, past the kick-boxing bar and past the remnants of last night's binge drinking. As bodies shuffled back and forth, moving in both directions on the street, one stood still in the middle of it. I didn't have to look at his face to know it was him.

"Hello, Bobby," I said as I approached. It didn't matter that his actual name was probably some combination of syllables a moron like me could never pronounce. He already knew I called him Bobby. He knew everything I knew.

"The Big Guy . . . here for the weed!" he said.

"That is correct," I responded.

I didn't know why I bothered to communicate verbally since Bobby was already in my head. He knew my next move, my every thought.

I reached out my hand and passed him 1,500 Thai baht. He appeared so small at this point he was almost imperceptible. He was more a concept of a man as opposed to a regular human, a dissipating enigma, slowly fading away to nothing.

"For you Big Guy!" he said and passed me a perfectly square block of hardened weed. I waited for sirens to start up, for Bobby to pull off his Thai drug dealer mask and have a Thai police officer mask on.

"It's the good stuff," he said, and I knew it was. No matter where you go in the world, every drug dealer refers to their weed as being the best. No matter how shitty it is, no matter how dry or wet, it's always *the good stuff*.

I unzipped a side pocket on my shorts and put the block in. When I looked back up, the town fluttered by as it usually did. New arrivals walked with their big back packs and heads on a swivel. Thai locals sold food and hats and had monkeys you could pet. The party kids were still in bed, but some who hadn't called it quits yet stumbled around like curious zombies. No one was coming for me. I wasn't going to prison. I had a block of dry weed and was on a party island. Things weren't so bad.

Bobby gave a little wink and walked away, blending into the crowd, just a guy trying to make a living, surviving in this harsh world.

VIEW FROM THE TOP IN CHEAP FLIP-FLOPS

We're no Ironman contestants but we *are* relatively fit in an average, 30-somethings-don't-survive-on-Mars-bars kind of way. We're outdoorsy. We like hiking, biking, kayaking, and even hit up the gym from time to time. I practise yoga and Mike likes to pretend he's George Foreman in our backyard. Most of our travel days include walks of up to 20 kilometres. It's never really a planned thing, it just kind of happens. It's a great way to explore an area and admire its nooks and crannies. Sometimes our feet are tired by the end of the day, but never are we celebrating a physical triumph deserving of anything more than a cold beer or an extra helping of tiramisu. Whether we're in a city like Los Angeles or an ecotourism mecca like Costa Rica, we always seem to get our "steps in."

It was May. Rainy season in Costa Rica. Many travellers are deterred by the rainy season, but for us it meant cheaper hotel rooms and fewer crowds. It would rain every day, usually for about an hour, coming down so hard and unexpected it felt like a practical joke. But then it would stop and be beautiful again.

We had rented a Jeep for this 10-day trip and took advantage of some muddy off-roading during these downpours. In an instant, the ground went from sturdy to slippery and made whatever adventure we were on feel a little more monster-truck rally.

We were staying in a little town called Arenal at a place called Green Lagoon Wellness Lodge. There was free breakfast, a pool and a view that made staying in feel like we were characters in a guidebook. Although there were plenty of local tours and attractions, we were intrigued by a particular hiking trail that was only accessible from our hotel grounds. A secret trail, you might say. Anything secret or sacred in a foreign country (or in your own backyard for that matter) feels both dangerous and magical. Like finding the portal to Narnia, or the boarding gate to Hogwarts. We didn't have this hike on our itinerary, but part of travel excitement is leaving room for the unknown.

We sat with our feet immersed in the cool hotel swimming pool water and decided we'd explore the Cerro Chato Trail that was sacred to the locals. The woman at the front desk advised (or rather warned) that the hike was not for the faint of heart. It was quite challenging, and we should be prepared for some more technical sections than we might be used to. She said it wasn't recommended AT ALL in rainy season and was extremely steep, unpredictable, and unstable in certain areas.

I don't know if we were cocky or confident, but these words did not resonate. "We're from Canada," we told ourselves. We've hiked Peggy's Cove in a snowstorm and trekked the arduous cobblestone streets in Old Montreal half drunk and weighed down with full bellies of Schwartz's smoked meat. We could do anything. We'd be back in a couple of hours and go for another dip in the pool before dinner. It would be a chance to stretch our legs and keep our bodies from succumbing to those extra pounds that seem inevitable when on vacation.

We didn't have a map or even an inkling of what the hike was going to be. I think someone said it was more than a 1,000-metre climb, but that didn't translate into "possible or not possible" in our minds. Was that far? Was it steep? How high is 1,000 metres? How many school busses or football fields lined up back-to-back did that equate to? In the absence of this understanding, we simply ignored the number. Maybe 1,000 wasn't a lot. Like getting 1,000 grains of salt in a bag, or $1,000 left to go on your mortgage.

We knew once we got to the top, there would be a view of a dormant volcano. There is an active volcano in Arenal, appropriately named the Arenal volcano, but the sister peak had been inactive for years and was now a giant crater filled with glimmering turquoise water. We needed to see it.

We wore shorts, tank-tops, flip-flops, and backpacks. When I was younger, I used to make fun of those couples that dressed alike. At home in Nova Scotia, couples that do this can almost always be found wearing the same thick denim jeans, a free T-shirt from a case of beer, and bright white "dad" sneakers. I swore I would never be one of these people, but here we were, in the middle of tropical paradise in our striped tank tops, cut-off shorts, MEC backpacks, and black, squishy TEVA flip-flops.

The sole of the TEVA "Mush" sandal is made from a combination of Play-Doh and kitten bellies. We wear them on every trip and eventually they mould to the grooves of your feet (even my wildly weird set of toes that are all the same length). By the end of this hike, we would be locally known as "The Canadians who were hiking in flip-flops."

The trailhead was visible from the pool that I was dangling my 10 equal-length toes in. Despite the alleged difficulty, it had been luring us in for the past few days and we agreed together, it was conquerable.

It was a clear, sunny day and the first section of the trail looked like a meadow where you might stumble upon a sleeping sheep or Cinderella. It was a storybook of clover, wildflowers and buzzing bees that surely didn't sting but rather gave soft, dewy kisses upon your smiling cheeks. Inside our backpacks, we had one filled water bottle, sunscreen from a now bankrupt K-Mart store, books we thought we'd have time to read, but that only added unnecessary weight, and fresh sliced watermelon for a snack.

For the first half-hour of the walk, I felt like we were on a movie set for *Little House on the Prairie*. There were wise, old trees covered in moss and what appeared to be farming fences that were taken down to invite passersby to enjoy the scenery. The higher we climbed, the more elaborate and impressive the view of the town below became. We meandered through the pixies and sprites, immersed in the ease and beauty around us.

About an hour into the pioneer path, the terrain shifted. The landscape went from *Anne of Green Gables* to the Eye of Mordor. Like a line was drawn through the land, we had one mush sandal in a fairy tale and the other in a fantasy horror. The boulder-sized rocks looked like giant pieces of salt and pepper, dropped at random from the angry Gods above. The stable farmland had transitioned into a muddier, slicker, steeper, narrowing pathway that led only from one sharp and glistening rock to the next.

We travelled on this terrain for quite some time. Our water was about half gone. The heat wasn't too bad that day, but the higher we climbed, the thicker the air became. We felt like we were exploring parts of the earth that had never been touched before, the rawness of the mossy ground like a hobbit community under new settlement. Each of our steps was intentional and focused, navigating through the spicy landscape. It was a constant uphill climb. No switchbacks. Just a straight ascent up a steep and slippery mountain. Intermittent breaks allowed the lactic acid in our legs time for a quick nap. Each step required staring at the ground and placing our foot exactly on an established bullseye to keep our balance. Thankfully, our $17 Jell-O-soled sandals attached to our feet by the equivalent to a flimsy grocery bag strap were the ideal vessels to overcome the tumultuous terrain.

We had climbed a fair distance and assumed we were somewhere near the summit. It had to be at least halfway. It was hard to tell. We ran into a couple on their way down the mountain face. They stopped to say hello and looked judgementally at our sandals. We looked in return at their hiking boots, outfitted with industrial-grade laces and ankle support. They held hiking poles and wore Tilly hats to keep the sun off their face. I wanted to show them the (expired) SPF 15 sunscreen in my bag to prove we were responsible too. Instead, we exchanged a polite nod.

The trail's landscape began to evolve again. We didn't know where we were, how much further we had to go or what the terrain ahead would bring. We knew we had about two tablespoons of water left, we were approaching an incredibly steep section and our flip flops had a thickening layer of mud on the bottom, creating an ever slicker and unstable surface than the ground itself.

We could see another smiling couple approaching us through the winding trail ahead. We grew hopeful they could offer some intel on what we could only assume would be the final leg ahead.

"You're about halfway!" they said with good cheer and an expression of satisfaction that exists only on a descent. They added, "Oh hey! You're the Canadians hiking in their flip-flops! We've heard about you guys!" as they pointed in amusement at our muddy, unprotected, fly-bitten feet. We didn't know if we should feel complimented or foolish but we laughed along with them and told them we were doing just fine.

We were not fine.

"Half fucking way!" I said in disbelief, looking to Mike for his conclusions on the likelihood of our survival. We had to be more than halfway. We'd been going up for three hours!

We sat down on a fallen log. The incline and terrain ahead looked as though it was built for a giant. There were times already when Mike was standing behind me, pushing up on my butt as my legs were too short to stretch between the steps that had been surely carved out by dinosaurs. We took out the last hope of hydration and sanity from Mike's backpack—the bag of sliced watermelon we had taken from breakfast that morning and stashed away for emergency purposes. Emergencies like this one.

On another equally sweaty hike we had discovered that a bag of watermelon in a hot climate is the equivalent to Mario eating mushrooms. The fresh, sweet juice offers more than a liquid snack, it offers hope and, I believe, new cells and tissue.

TRAVEL TIP: *Fresh fruit in a hot climate is the hydration equivalent to steroids for Jose Canseco.*

We shared a few squares of the pink medicine and had a heart-to-heart that we will remember for the rest of our marriage. It was a moment of encouragement and determination that to this day, I feel defines the commitment we have to each other. We talked about how far we had come and that if it was another four minutes or four hours, we would get through this hike together. The hike had become a metaphor for our relationship and life ahead of us. We would get each other there. If we had to carry or drag one another, we would both be triumphant on this climb. We observed the surrounding flora and fauna. We could feel the thickness of the tropical heat, the warm, sweet air filling our lungs. We now understood what "in the thick of it" really meant. We had become one with the land, immersed in the forest like carrots in a stew. There were endless examples of synergy and symbiotic growth: ants crawling up vines, vines crawling up moss, moss crawling up trees. We were encased by greenery and chatty birds. We were surrounded in life and survival. We let the glucose from the watermelon run through our veins, the sounds and spirit of the rainforest fill our souls, and words of encouragement exchanged to each other fill our hearts.

We would finish this hike today. We would do it without water, without knowledge, and without hiking boots. We would finish this hike because we had each other.

We grabbed thick vines and used them as rope to pull us up the inclining rock face, Tarzan's genetics paling in comparison. Our quads burned with each methodical step forward. We were silent now, almost meditative. We were driven and focused and needed to conserve our energy for the sake of endurance. Every foot hold slow and manoeuvred, knowing that the throne-like steps were only growing taller and wider as the trail progressed.

And then suddenly, as if no time had passed at all, we were at the top. At the very time we were forced to mull over our choices between trudging on or turning back, we were unknowingly just steps away from completing the hike.

We had heard rumours, folklore even, that if you made it to the top of this mountain, you would be gifted with a distant view of a lake filled with turquoise water bluer than the lapis stone that peppered the very lands that we walked. It was a rare sighting, however. The elevated viewpoint at which we stood was almost always foggy and dewy, erasing the view of even a few meters ahead. It was as though the moment our battered and dirty feet stepped onto the summit, the curtain of fog was gracefully pulled back like a veil over a bride's ready-to-be-kissed face. A secret fairy-tale lake was revealed, writhing in spellbinding power and crystal blue glimmer. It was breathtaking. Or maybe we were simply breathless from the effort it took to get there. Either way, it was an unwrapped gift that was waiting for our arrival. We high-fived, laughed, and celebrated our accomplishment.

We heard footsteps behind us, the sound of hiking boots trudging through the intricate Costa Rican ecosystem. And upon a final bow, the curtain of fog covered over the lake once again, hiding the magic of the secret lake for the next set of chosen explorers to be blessed by her beauty.

GOT THE GAMBIA:

Love Story #1

I suppose it all started when I first got the email. I was playing every possible show that I could, trying to get my band's name out there: Tuesdays at dive bars, Sundays opening for karaoke. I was sleeping on couches and floors and didn't have a cellphone. If someone wanted to get in touch with me quickly, I had to be within yelling distance.

An email came in about a short-notice show in three days. It was an art fundraiser for the Nova Scotia Gambia Association. I didn't know what a Gambia was, but it was capitalized and sounded like a disease so I said yes. I didn't know if the girl who emailed me—Kristen Herrington—had Gambia or not, but I felt sorry for her in case she did and agreed to play it for no pay.

On a freezing cold February 16th night, me and my bandmate Bruce went to the show. It was the coldest day of the year. I walked into the bar with snot dripping down my red face and teeth chattering. That's when I met Kristen. When I first saw her, she smiled so big and warm I thought everything in the world was good and always would be. She had nice boobs, too. We talked and laughed and seemed to get along really well. I managed not to say anything too stupid and she responded positively to everything I said, so it was a win.

I told her I'd add her on Facebook. She said we might as well exchange numbers in case either of us needed anything before the show. I said I didn't have a phone so I gave her Bruce's number to get in touch with me.

I added her online that night and we talked every day for a month.

She said she liked my grammar. I guess I'm pretty good at *your* and *you're* and know *there*, *their*, and *they're* inside and out. I told her I wrote a book and started sending her chapters. She was the first person to read what I had written, and that made me nervous. Especially with the nice boobs and all. She'd write back funny emails that made me smile. I thought it would be fun to have those conversations in person.

On St. Paddy's day we got together for the first time. Kristen baked muffins but burned the hell out of them. I didn't care because someone had made me muffins and I like burned things anyway.

She had rented a movie called *Happiness Runs*. For a first date movie, most people typically try to get something easygoing. Something that isn't controversial or pushing any hot-topic buttons. It's hard to describe the weirdness of this movie, but it involved a hippie commune teen sex cult with themes of suicide and drug use. I didn't know if she was half crazy and into that kind of thing but I didn't really care. We laughed and made fun of it the entire time and I thought to myself that I could get used to this.

If all girls who had Gambia were like her, I was thinking of joining the association.

MY WORST POOP

It was the worst confession I had to make in my marriage. Mike and I were soaking in a warm bath one night discussing future plans, goals and dreams; all the things you do in a cozy tub. I felt it was time I shared a secret I had been keeping. Something that had happened years before and had caused a great deal of grief. Something I feared may change the way he looked at me but needed to come out. It was about a dramatic—or possibly traumatic—poop I had had.

Travel pooping may be an overlooked subject in guide books or advice blogs, but it's something we're all faced with. Travel pooping—not to be confused with pooping while travelling—can be the most memorable story you bring home. Most travellers, particularly those who journey through countries with obscure foods, questionable water, and scalding climates, will know exactly what I mean. Bathroom strategizing and pre-planning is essential. Knowing a bathroom's proximity is important; having toilet paper on-person is imperative. I learned why this was the case due to an unfortunate circumstance that took place in the early years of our dating.

This is the same story I told Mike (for the first time) that night while sitting in the bathtub together. It's a story I had never told anyone. Even at the time that it originally happened, when we were already madly in love, I didn't feel I could share this with him. I judged myself too much. But shit stories are inevitable and unfortunately, plentiful. And if we were going to spend a lifetime travelling together, it was time to come clean on what I had done.

We were travelling from Chiang Mai, Thailand, to a smaller northern community called Pai. It's a popular destination, typically appealing to a younger, hipster-type crowd. While the town itself is lovely, the trip to get there is not. Passengers are warned before boarding the eight-seater cube van that the road is VERY twisty and turny. It's a 509-metre climb up a mountain, stretched out over 293 switchbacks from bottom to top. We sat at the back of the cube van with our bags and other luggage stashed under the seat in front of us. There was an eclectic mix of travellers, many speaking different languages but sharing the same sense of nausea. After about 188 turns, one of the dudes in front of us couldn't take it any longer. He vomited ALL OVER our stashed away luggage. From that day on, my purse—which took the brunt of the trauma—would be referred to as "the puke bag."

But that's not the gross part of this story. The gross part happens shortly after the puke when the van driver pulled over for the sole scheduled bathroom break. There are many of these roadside stops throughout Thailand. A few vendors sell fried plantain or bags of fresh fruit. Every so often you'd get someone making hot soup or barbeque meat. The food always cost less than $2 and is the best you've ever had. The stops are usually outfitted with public washrooms too. A biscuit-sized Thai woman sits at the entry of the cement pisshole, selling squares of toilet paper prior to your permitted entry. A toilet toll, so to speak. It was always cheap and always worth it. Because you almost always have the shits while travelling.

On this day, there was no biscuit-sized Thai woman selling toilet paper at the washroom. I charged through the opening in the cement wall and dove headfirst into a bathroom stall. Muscles I didn't know I had started contracting involuntarily. It was both a mental and physical battle NOT to shit myself as a grown woman. In a foreign country when you're hours away from your own private bathroom it was even worse. My pants could not come off fast enough, as poop-anxiety-sweat ran down the nape of my neck. It was the kind where you start self-talking, "Almost there. You're in the bathroom. Just one more second! Hold it the fuck in!!!"

Hovering over the carved-out hole in a sumo squat, I felt a rush of relief wash over me. One more day without crapping myself in public! I looked over to grab the toilet paper. My instincts told me the paper was just an arm's reach away. It wasn't. The only thing in sight was the dirty plastic ice cream pail, filled with water that you used to "flush" the shit down the hole. This is the Thai way. There was no toilet paper because the biscuit woman was not there to sell me any.

I heard the van driver honk the horn. That's the signal for "get back here immediately or I'm leaving without you."

My short sense of relief skyrocketed back to maximum panic. This is not a pee in the woods and do a cute little wiggle and everything is good kind of situation. It was the opposite of that. I HAD to have toilet paper. I started digging around in the puke bag, desperate to find a scrap of something that past, prepared traveller me stashed away in effort to be nice to future, has-the-shits me. I had nothing. I was still hovering in a shit-squat, small pieces of poop debris flying about as I frantically emptied all the inner pockets of the vomit covered bag. I was going to be left behind in a Thai bathroom with only a faded shit bucket and my own disgrace. Amidst my thrashing, I noticed one more item in the cement cell of a bathroom stall. A second, cheap plastic bucket that was a garbage can. It was filled with used toilet paper from days past.

Even now, I wish the story from this point on went differently. I still struggle with self-judgment and shame about what happened next. But desperation permits actions that we would not otherwise take. I had no choice.

I waddled over to the bucket to see if I could find a wad of tissue that had clean ends—the parts that are used for gripping, not wiping. The parts that are still white and on the fringe of other people's bathroom stories. I managed to tear off one to two squares' worth from a few separate balls. Cumulatively, I had enough that I could pinch the small, Q-tip size worth of other peoples' toilet paper between my fingers. I did a surface wipe with it. Just enough that it would only leave streak marks and not chunks in my underwear. It was survival. It was the lesser of the evils.

The van's engine was running, Mike started yelling for me.

I ran out of the bathroom, filled with horror and humiliation. I felt like I had just committed a crime. I could never tell Mike what happened. I was afraid of what he might think of me. I wanted him to still find me attractive and sexy. This would surely destroy that honeymoon phase we were enjoying. The blood had drained from my face and confidence from my psyche. I sat quietly, holding the puke bag close to my body as a way of covering up my embarrassment. I swore then that I would always carry extra toilet paper with me. I do it now just going to the grocery store, hanging clothes on the line, and getting a snack out of the fridge. That situation will never happen to me again.

> **TRAVEL TIP:** *Always, 100 per cent of the time, no matter what, bring toilet paper with you wherever you go.*

BREAKING THE NEWS TO PARENTS

No matter where we go in the world, Dad will react like we're going to a war zone in Afghanistan. In his head, as soon as we get off the plane we're dodging bullets, evading landmines, and diving straight into the uncertain depths of "no man's land." Every place other than rural Nova Scotia might as well be some version of apocalyptic hell.

Mom is the opposite. "Oh my . . . it sounds like so much fun," she'd say upon hearing news of us going to Syria during the civil war, or "I heard there's such great food in the jungles of Papua New Guinea!"

When we decided we were going to Colombia, we realized one way or another we'd have to break it to our parents. We put more planning into how we were going to tell my dad than we did the trip itself. We calculated and scrutinized, made graphs, pros and cons lists, created mock scenarios and rated them on a scale of 1 to CONNIPTION FIT. It took us a while, but we developed what we believed to be the perfect plan.

We went home for Christmas. That alone makes my mom's year. My other brothers were both away, so we immediately had bonus points from being the only kids at home. We figured it was necessary to buy a REALLY GOOD gift that year. After my grandmother died in 2000, my parents inherited her floor model TV. Even then, it was both out of date and on its last legs. It was giant and bulky with horrible reception and weighed as much as an elephant. Even though Dad watches sports every day, he's too cheap to buy something even a tad bit better. "Works great!" he'll say as some fuzzy figure slightly resembling LeBron James scurries up and down the court, the announcer's descriptions of the game the only real way to tell what's happening. For Christmas we'd buy them a new TV. A 45-inch flat screen at that. It would be big and clear and LeBron's muscles would be so definitive you'd swear he was right there in the living room.

We knew that to pull off the Colombia reveal we had to go all out. Colombia was—at one point in time—*actually* the most dangerous place on earth. Not just *a* dangerous place. *THE MOST* dangerous. In Medellin, where we were going, every time a person left their house in the '80s they assumed they would die. They'd kiss their kids and say goodbye, expecting a random bomb or stray bullet to end it all. Even though the city and country has made remarkable strides away from this, that kind of thing sticks with a man like my dad. THE MOST DANGEROUS PLACE ON EARTH. And that's where we were going.

The plan was a six-step process.

1. Food: Stuff Dad with turkey dinner—his favourite meal—till he's in a comatose-like state. With the tryptophan in the turkey, he'd be groggy and slightly calmed down. Earlier in the day, we'd hide all his favourite mid-afternoon snacks (plain chips, Bits and Bites, etc.) so he couldn't fill up on them and be forced to eat excessive amounts of turkey.

2. Awesome present: Give Dad the giant, brand new TV, hook it up for him, and put basketball on so he could see the significant improvement that this would make in his life. In his eyes, a flat-screen TV of that size is worth probably $10,000. He would think that we broke the bank completely for him.

3. Start talking about first aspect of trip: Costa Rica (key in on it being the *happiest* place on earth). Talk about the yoga retreat Kristen was going to and how I was going to work on a new book. Since we'd been to Costa Rica before and somehow magically survived, it had been deemed at least a little bit safer than an axe fight.

4. Kristen's white chocolate pumpkin truffles: For the last five Christmases, Kristen had made the most delicious truffles any human had ever tasted. Dad typically fits as many as he can into his mouth at a time and lets the party begin. "They ever fuckin' good!"

he'll say, his mouth watering and agape. At this critical juncture in time, as the sweet sugary bliss dissolved in his mouth we'd move on to step five.

5. Briefly mention we're *also* going to Colombia.

6. Disneyworld and Uncle Jimmy: To end the trip, we'd be going to Disney. I know this would likely confuse Dad more than anything and take his mind off what he'd just heard. A grown man going to Disney? Isn't that for kids and girls? Was there something wrong with my son? And while at Disney, we'd get to spend a night with Uncle Jimmy who spent the winters just outside of Orlando.

We travelled to Cape Breton from Halifax, TV in the back seat, truffles ready, and our plan mentally mapped out to perfection. When we arrived, Mom was waiting at the door and hugged us both, her eyes lighting up with joy. Dad shook Kristen's hand and looked at me. "Come down to the basement . . . we gotta get rid of the old hot water heater."

He'd been waiting weeks for this. Reinforcements. The only thing on his mind was moving that tank. He *could* have asked one of his friends. Even a neighbour or God forbid a brother. But in his eyes, the fact that he didn't play a direct role in their fruition as a living entity meant he couldn't in a million years ask them for a favour. He'd sooner light himself on fire than ask for help from people he's known his entire life. In exchange for my existence in the flesh, the least I could do was help out my poor old father.

The words couldn't get out of his mouth fast enough. I didn't even get a chance to put my bags down and I was lifting a heavy—and, for some reason, greased up—metal tank. "I think there's still a lot of water in it," I said. "If we drain that out it will be a hell of a lot easier."

Dad just shook his head. "No, that takes too much time . . . it's not heavy, just awkward."

It was actually both very heavy and very awkward. "Not heavy, just awkward" has been the male go-to for thousands of years. No man will ever admit that something is in fact, heavy. It's always just the shape of it, the fact that there's no real spot to grip it properly. No item ever moved by a man has ever been heavy. The circumstances around moving it, always,

100 per cent of the time, the issue.

I wrapped my arms around the greasy metal tank filled with water, bent my back the way you're not supposed to, and Dad did the same. Kristen was upstairs likely having a cup of tea and basking in the compliments Mom would be showering upon her. "She's an awkward fucker!" Dad said as we began the ascent of the stairs. My back was already hurting and my knees always hurt so they just hurt more.

After the four-hour drive, before getting a glass of water or having a leak, the thing I least wanted to be doing was lifting a heavy, greasy metal tank. But I knew this would give us bonus points. If I got the tank out, it would aid in our upcoming master plan.

So I lifted it. I could feel my back losing years of uprightness but I didn't care. Every step was a struggle. The fact that we're both well over six feet and had to duck on the winding basement stairs made it both easy and fun. We were sweating profusely and Dad, as usual, cursing like a lunatic, "YOU ALL-AMERICAN COCKSUCKER!" he yelled. I had thought that in my 35 years I had heard all my father's possible combinations of swearing. This was a new one. I was kind of impressed. Dad had picked up something new. It was nice to see he was still capable, in his 60s, of learning new things to be used in his day to day life.

We finally got it up the stairs, through the inside porch door, through the outside door, onto the deck, and put it down.

"That wasn't so bad," Dad said.

"Why'd you just curse for 40 minutes straight and act like the world was ending?"

"Yeah whatever . . . gotta get the new one in now."

We went to the barn to find the sparkling clean, shiny new hot water tank. We latched onto it, expecting the struggle of ample weight to once again strain our backs. It was like lifting a feather. There was no water in it.

"Shoulda took the water out of the other one, eh?" Dad said.

This is pretty much how all jobs we've ever done had gone. I initially suggest something to make it easier, he doesn't listen, then realizes upon conclusion that my suggestion would have made it exponentially simpler.

The next day and a half we got to all the talk that parents and their kids have on their infrequent visits: How are things going? How's work?

Why don't you have kids yet? When are you thinking about having kids? Etc.

When Christmas Day arrived, we were like Olympic athletes who'd prepared for something their entire life. We executed the plan to perfection. Dad legitimately thought he won the lotto in giving him a $299, 45-inch flat screen. "Look how fuckin' clear it is!" he said with enthusiasm. "You can even see the score!"

On the old floor model, the dimensions of the screen weren't compatible with the new-age technology, and the score—if on the top, bottom or side of the screen—was cut out.

Without his afternoon snacks, Dad dove into the turkey head first. I could almost see the tryptophan seeping into his bloodstream with every bite.

When we started to talk about the trip, we pounded out the positive statistics about Costa Rica: stable democracy, strong economy, stunning microclimates, so safe they don't even have an army, and so on. Dad wasn't really paying much attention. He was groggy and veritably solidifying his opinion of Steph Curry being a "hot dog" with the newfound definition on the big screen.

As Kristen talked about her yoga retreat and the great group of women she'd be doing it with, I handed Dad five of the white-chocolate truffles. Even though she'd made them the last four years and they had become a solidified part of our Christmas tradition, Dad was still shocked. "These those same things as last year?" he said with amazement.

"Even better this year!" I said as he started to shove them into his mouth.

I took a seat on the couch beside Kristen and elbowed her lightly. She knew it was time. After a good 45 minutes of focusing on Costa Rica, I began:

"And after that we're going to Colombia for a bit."

Immediately following my two-second mention of the most dangerous place on earth, Kristen piped up with "And we'll end the trip with going to Disney and to see Uncle Jimmy!"

I saw Dad's head turn towards us slowly. His cheeks were puffed with the surplus of chocolate balls in his mouth. His eyes were droopy, and I think I could see drool forming on the edges of his lips. He wanted to say something. He wanted to contest. But he was too far gone. Like a drugged-up tiger at a petting zoo, you know it wants to rip the heads of those children and eat their organs. But the fight is taken out of them. They can't do anything but sit there and let the kids get what they want.

"Colombia?" he said softly as he swallowed the most delicious dessert he'd ever had.

On the TV, I could hear the crowd cheering and announcer raising his voice as the intensity of the game and moment rose.

Steph Curry hit a long three-pointer and started his patented celebration dance. Dad turned back towards his new TV, focused in and shook his head.

"Hot dog," he said to no one in particular.

I knew we were safe.

Burned Muffins and Cults:
Love Story #2

I haven't been on many dates in my life. Maybe it's because most of the men who I've been in relationships with I've met organically, at a party or through a friend. The only thing my generation swiped left was the sweat from our brow. Most relationships were built without ever feeling "datey." Maybe I just didn't get asked out much. Either way, I felt inexperienced when I met Michael.

I had been talking to Mike online for a month. We met at an art fundraiser I had hosted, where he unknowingly saved the day. His chivalry made for a good first impression and so I connected online to thank him again and let him know how much I was enjoying the CD he had gifted me. Throughout the weeks since our first encounter, Mike had shared chapters of his first book with me, revealing a timeline of his life. He was working on a memoir that told the story of his band's adventures, hardships, shenanigans, and coming of age. I learned that in his 20s he had set an old couch on fire with gasoline in the middle of a military baseball field. I knew he had a cousin named James and his mom really liked cats (she had seven). I discovered he lived for music, liked grilled cheese cheeseburgers and kicking things that were really high up. He seemed odd in a way I felt myself to be. He also sent me a few of his YouTube videos. One where he was doing an operation on a robot while wearing a space suit and one where he sings a revised theme song for the movie *Snakes on a Plane* that goes, "Get these motherfucking snakes off this motherfucking plane," in a beautifully tender falsetto. His dark, curly hair was slicked back and he wore a crisp suit and a neck tie. He told me he filmed it at a particular piano store because the owner was blind and couldn't see what he was doing.

I knew enough to really like him.

Mike was living in Cape Breton throughout these weeks of corresponding on Facebook. His hometown, Inverness, wasn't as famous as it has grown to be now, but from the pictures he sent (or rather, the ones that I creeped), it looked serene. He said that he was taking a trip from the island and coming to Halifax for St. Paddy's Day. He would be staying with James.

My heart fluttered a little as we casually agreed that, "maybe we would see each other in person while he was in the area." I felt as though he liked me too, but I had dated musician types before (nobody had yet warned me not to) and I knew they lived a transient and independent lifestyle. I paused and realized, so did I. Perhaps mothers had warned their sons about girls like me . . .

Our first date was planned for March 17, 2011. Hoping to avoid the sea of green vomit and "Kiss Me, I'm Irish" T-shirts, I asked Mike if he'd like to hang out at my place. Neither of us were all that interested in food colouring in our beer or restaurants overcrowded with leprechauns and four-leaf clovers bought from the Dollar Store. Plus, I felt a little more in control if we were at my place. My apartment was the classic university basement rental with a left-behind microwave and toilet whose handle you had to jiggle. But I had a few neat books and a set of dishes that matched. I was confident this would be enough to impress a guy who once killed a rat, indoors, with a sword.

When I got nervous, which happened exactly the moment I woke up that day, I called my best friend Jessie to ask for her advice. She had more dating experience than I did. She had more everything experience than I did, and I trusted her expert opinion. She was in the food and hospitality industry and had made the accurate, universal observation that men liked food. As a starting point, I should have something to eat on hand, she suggested. I felt unprepared. This seemed like such an obvious oversight on my part. Food! Of course. Always have food for guests. I had nine boxes of cereal and five different kinds of cheese, but didn't think those things went together. For bonus points, Jessie clarified, I could bake something. This would make my musty basement apartment smell like cinnamon and childhood. Things that men like.

I had a pre-packaged muffin mix that was only outdated by a year and a muffin tin that my ma was going to throw away but that I asked to keep instead. It was tar-black and would be the vehicle to a successful first date.

Mike said he would be there at noon. It was an unusually warm spring day in Halifax, which meant that I had to come up with an outfit that wasn't in my regular winter rotation. Picking out clothes for a first date is one of life's meanest moments. Many women can relate to having a closet so full of clothing that there's a good chance you've broken a fire marshal's code. I'm surprised my landlord wasn't charging me for a second occupant. But in that moment, I was the Paper Bag Princess with only tattered rags and paper bags to throw over my now sweating and flailing body. A flurry of self-judgment and concern washed over me. By the end of the selection process there were so many piles of clothes strewn about I felt like I had just rummaged through an avalanche for a corpse.

I settled for a long-sleeve, blue cotton Adidas dress. It was comfortable but still a dress so it felt dressy *enough* but not like I was trying too hard. "This old thing? Oh yeah, I think I just got this at Value Village (true) and just threw it on before you got here (lie)," I would say if Mike complimented it. I wondered what he would have on. I wondered if guys went through this much agony preparing for first dates. Would he wear a dress shirt? Would it be ironed or something he bought new?

My plan was to put the muffins in the oven shortly before noon so that they would be fresh at just the right time. My apartment would smell of cinnamon about 30 minutes into our date and would act as a bonus feature to how awesome it is at Kristen's place.

Mike was almost an hour late. We still disagree on this detail. He feels he was right on time (he truly is a punctual person) and as I'm sure is becoming clear, I was quite nervous. Either way, his unknown whereabouts and lack of cellphone only made me more jittery. Was I being stood up by the guy who taped Faxe beer to his hands and wore a jacket from 1993 with someone else's names sewn on the sleeve?

It was 12:50 p.m. Amidst my panic, I was distracted by the smell of smoke. Was someone having a campfire in downtown Halifax on a March afternoon? It was St. Paddy's Day. People do crazy things on St. Paddy's Day. Suddenly my smoke detector started screaming. That long, obnoxious, foghorn cry to let you know you fucked up.

The goddamn muffins.

They had been in the oven almost twice as long as the $1.99 bag had instructed. They were now lava mountains, spitting fire and soot throughout my kitchen. I cracked the oven door and a tidal wave of smoke slapped my already sweaty face. I felt my eyelashes singe and mascara melt into my tear ducts. I grabbed the now blacker tin pan and threw it, with its 12 bowling ball muffins, on the counter and launched open my kitchen window. My apartment felt more like a horror movie. It smelled of char and decay, not cinnamon and desire. I was running around, hot and anxious. My skin was dewy, my dress wet with armpit sweat, and my hair now thrown up in a messy ponytail.

I heard a knock at my door.

I froze in the middle of my kitchen floor. I was exactly the opposite of what I had hoped to be in this moment. I was a disaster. I looked like I had been kidnapped and made to run home after my escape from a psychopath's windowless cube van. My apartment had just been on fire, maybe it still was, and was now colder than a small town arena as all of the windows were open. I had only blackened bullets to offer and I was painfully aware that Mike had to knock a second time at my door.

I yelled "Come in," which sounded like a desperate shrill of despair, screamed from the lungs of a tortured demon.

"Hello," Mike called in a calm voice, his neck craned down as all six foot four of his body crept down the stairs into the dragon's den of smoke.

"Hi," I replied sheepishly, under a haze that was now burning my eyes and making my poorly applied makeup run.

Mike didn't comment on the smell, the smoke, or the situation in general. He just smiled and shifted his weight a little awkwardly but seemed generally happy to see me. He was wearing a tight white Dole banana T-shirt and a pair of faded swimming trunks. He also had on a multicoloured ball cap and sneakers with laces I think weren't the original set. I don't believe he had clothing Everest on his bed at home.

I asked if he wanted to come in and have a seat on the couch. I had rented us a movie to watch—one that I had spent almost as long picking out as I had my outfit—

and hoped it would somehow distract from the simultaneous hot and cold that seemed to be happening but wasn't being talked about.

In those days, movie rentals were still a thing. In Halifax there was a store called Video Difference, which supplied a steady stream of both blockbusters and indie obscurities. I wanted to rent something "cool" so went to the indie section. Without really knowing someone, it's hard to choose a film you'll both appreciate. Even after a decade of being together, we still have to have a conversation about what movie we're in the mood for. I now know Mike generally likes films about boxing, war, or Vikings. I generally like movies starring Jennifer Aniston, puppies, or also Vikings, but for different reasons than Mike. The movie I selected had none of these things. The cover and brief description on the movie jacket made it look quirky and had reviews written by people I had never heard of, but I wanted to prove to an artist like Mike that I *too* was interesting and intelligent. That I "got" high art. That I could dissect and critique an independent take on alternative film. That I could find a philosophical metaphor that was surely the undertone of this indie film rented from an indie store that I was hip enough to know about. I was an artist too, after all. A painter, not a musician, but was certainly privy to creative obscurities, self-expression, and the unpredictable life that artists like us knowingly sign up for. We had this in common at least.

We sat side by side on the most uncomfortable couch in the world. It was basically a collection of thick metal bars with some tissue paper sewn overtop. If you didn't sit exactly still in one particular spot, you would have a cross bar slam up between your butt cheeks.

"Umm, I made muffins but they're pretty burnt," I half-offered as the opening credits started to roll on my loaf of bread-sized television screen. I noticed there were some creepy scenes of teenagers burning things at a stake and I wanted to come up with a distraction. What the hell did I rent? The burned muffins were the best I had to offer at this point.

Much to my surprise and relief, his first bite was accompanied by a thumbs up and a grin. I would later learn that this was a guy who has survived for days off of mustard and pizza crusts, so in hindsight, burned, packaged muffins weren't such an epic fail after all.

Four muffins in, I felt more at ease. I think he actually DID like them. We chatted about Mike's hometown and I told him I had once been to Inverness. I had visited with three friends who I had tree-planted with that summer. One of the girls had a friend who lived there. We had watched the horse races, got food poisoning, went to a party, and had a bonfire at the beach where we were nearly struck by lightning. "I have a few pictures of that trip, actually," I said and pulled out a stack of photos from the shelf beside us. Flipping through, Mike recognized the faces of some locals and we giggled at the stories he shared about them. A photo popped up of the band we had seen at a bar in town called The Hoff.

"The people we were staying with took us to see this band," I said. "They told us we had to go, and we had the best time! We went to a party at the lead singer's house later too."

"Wait . . . that's my band! That's me!" Mike replied pointing to the blurry figure playing a guitar in the background. I found this somewhat serendipitous and felt a little butterfly be born out of the caterpillar that had been slowly walking me to first-date-death. Maybe this could be something. Maybe he would like me?

The movie on the other hand, I'm not sure either of us *liked*. In a nut-shell, it was about a teenage sex cult with plenty of drug consumption and violent ritualistic scenarios. On my checklist of first impressions, this was yet another epic fail. The movie lasted approximately 17 hours. Yet, at one point, fairly early on, the worst first date of all time took a turn for the better.

Once we had filled our bellies with charcoal, closed the windows, got the room temperature back up to a balmy arctic day, and balanced our butt cheeks like you would on the handles of bicycle, we let our real personalities shine.

My armpit-sweaty dress wasn't such a catastrophe sitting next to his faded shorts from the '80s. Before long we were in hysterics over the absurdity of the movie and making up our own commentary for each scene. Eventually, we even held hands, while maintaining our respective balancing postures on the Kleenex cage. I knew that if we could have fun under these circumstances, that we would have fun doing anything. I appreciated that Mike was able to see the humour in things and shared a mutual understanding that most situations in life aren't worth stressing about. I knew that it didn't matter what we did on our second date, I just hoped that there would be one.

BANG:

Travel Days Gone Wrong

We were waiting to board our first of three flights to Thailand when martial law was announced. I didn't really know what it was but figured it had something to do with karate and maybe Judge Judy. When I looked it up, I found out that it basically meant the military had taken over the government because something had gone to shit in the country. Seven seconds after it was declared, both our phones rang and our rural, small-town dads warned us we were marching into certain death. We weren't too concerned though. Realistically, it meant we weren't allowed out past 10 p.m. But when you're over 30, those are the hours typically reserved for lying in bed eating half-melted Mars bars and watching reruns of *Frasier* anyways. It looked like we could still go to beaches and curry would continue to be made, so it didn't have much effect on our plans.

After saying goodbye—and to our dads what they thought to be our *final* goodbye—we boarded our first flight to Newark. It would be a long day—23 hours in the air plus another seven running around airports—but the sheer excitement and adrenalin of the adventure to come would get us through. We held hands in our seat and smiled nonstop. This was our first big trip together. This was the start of it all.

We talked about everything to come: food, the majestic beauty we'd see, the roar and buzz of a city like Bangkok, and the chances of running into Tiger Woods who might be there visiting his Thai mother's family and would presumably be staying in the same $7 a night hotel as us. With travelling, the anticipation of what's ahead is an amazing thing. Just knowing that you're going elsewhere can get you through the hardest of times. It's a feeling of almost pure innocence. You don't know what will happen but know everything that should, surely will.

As the plane started its descent into Newark, the beauty of everything ahead on our minds, something strange happened. A sharp, instant pain in my forehead took over my entire being. Something in my head exploded. The only real way to describe it would be if a hot knife was jammed through my skull and into my brain, twisted aggressively, while the perpetrator of the stabbing sang "Bad Day" by Daniel Powter softly into my ears, only to realize that the perpetrator was in fact Daniel Powter himself.

I was instantly dizzy and covered in sweat. I grabbed Kristen's leg and said what anyone would in that circumstance: "I think the movie *Rambo* just happened in my brain."

I leaned forward and put my head on my knees. Kristen didn't know what was happening but saw I was in pain. All I was capable of was mumbling "Rambo" repeatedly.

She asked what she could do and I just said, "pills." She dug the Ibuprofen and Gravol out of her bag and I sat up. I realized my nose was bleeding. I played a million sports growing up, did all the stupid things boys do, and somehow had never gotten a bloody nose until that moment.

I took the pills and wiped the blood off my face. Like a near-dead football player being carted off the field on a stretcher, I gave Kristen the thumbs up to try to show I was fine but obviously wasn't.

The plane touched down. I had no idea what was happening but knew I felt like a piece of bread in the dishwasher. I just wanted to get off the plane, out of the crowded, hot space and into the beautiful, cool and relaxed utopia that is an airport.

There's that period of time before takeoff and after landing where the air stops circulating in the cabin. Airlines do this to make self-conscious people a little extra sweaty, sick people more nauseous, and for any babies not already crying to lose their shit. It heats up and every breath is an inhalation of body odour, farts that couldn't be held in any longer, and left behind roast-beef sandwiches people have to abandon because bringing cheap processed meat into a foreign country is for some reason the equivalent of a nuclear bomb in your luggage. I breathed in the weird union of smells and tried not to pass out.

The people in front of us were all extra slow. Any time you want someone to move fast that's always the case. Every time I've ever been in an emergency situation like having to buy Gatorade or pizza pockets at a corner store, with certainty, some 90-year-old woman in front of me has 6,000 scratch tickets to get scanned.

I shuffled my feet and moved sloth-like behind them. The urge to splash cold water on my face was irresistible. I was white and green at the same time and Kristen said I looked like if Powder and possessed Linda Blair had a child.

I slowly shuffled off, my head throbbing and my stomach turning. We were at the back of the plane because that's where we always end up. My bags were two giant cement blocks pulling me to the ground. I was a pathetic mess, weighed down and falling apart.

When we finally got off the plane, I made a beeline for the nearest bathroom. Blood dripped down my face but I couldn't wipe it because I was double fisted with luggage. I just let it drip like the disgusting human I'd become. There was a line of about a dozen people. The guy at the end turned around and saw me. The very second his eyes laid on me he jumped out of the way to let me ahead. Every. Single. Person. Did. They all moved. I mumbled and groaned and dragged my feet, barely able to lift them. I was a bleeding zombie and if they didn't move there was a high probability I may bite and infect them.

I got in and looked at myself in the mirror. Kristen's assessment was accurate. My face had crusted blood and all the telltale signs of a good meth binge—I would get out of that guy's way.

I splashed water on my face and felt the pills starting to kick in. The four Advil were lessening the pain, and the Gravol taking away the nausea.

When I got back to Kristen, she was busy trying to find a first aid station. We realized such a thing didn't exist in airports, or at least not in Newark in 2015.

We looked online. Well, we tried to look online. In our efforts to google "head exploding on plane" we found out that there was no internet—at least not in Newark in 2015.

It was time to board our next flight—a 14-hour and two-minute jaunt to Narita, Japan. I got on not knowing what happened to me. I didn't know if my brain was detonating or if it would happen again.

The flight had no movies and the seats were small. I thought there was a legitimate chance I might die. But I didn't care. We were on an adventure, our first real adventure. If I died in the air at least my love would be beside me. She could figure out what to do with my strangely coloured corpse.

I survived and slowly came around. We invented games, wrote notes, and made up stories about everyone on the plane. I realized how easy it was to do this with Kristen. She rubbed my head and fed me crackers and sandwiches when my appetite came around.

I didn't care about my head or the random squirts of blood. The girl I loved was with me and that was all that mattered. Tomorrow we'd be in Bangkok, a new city, a new adventure. And there was the possibility we'd be sharing a room with Tiger Woods too. That was pretty cool.

FAMILY REUNION ON A MOPED

Mike and I are okay on bicycles. I had a 10-speed when I was a teenager and learned fundamentals such as downshifting and how to attach holographic streamers to the handlebars. This felt like sufficient preparation to drive a small motorcycle around unknown backroads in Northern Thailand. Neither of us had ever ridden a moped but it was a popular activity in the town of Pai and looked easy enough. We were asked, but not required, to wear helmets. Aside from that, my only protective gear was a pair of cheap sandals and a one-piece cotton romper whose coverage rivalled only a bathing suit.

We did a thorough examination of the mini-mopeds we had rented to check for scratches or damage. Though the rental fee was reasonable, the collateral for accidents was not. We had heard that some local companies tried to blame tourists for damage on rentals, even though the returned bike was in the exact same condition as when it left. We snapped photos of the big scars and gouges that gleamed in the paint, wondering what history they came with and praying we would not add any more.

> **TRAVEL TIP:** *If you rent a vehicle while travelling, take a thorough look for existing damage before you take it off the lot. Take photos or video. This will protect you from any "misunderstandings" or discrepancies with staff and show that you're not a rookie in this game.*

It took a while to get comfortable. Between trying to stay balanced, follow memorized directions, and take in the scenery, eventually my knuckles faded from white-gripped to pink and relaxed. We travelled through farming communities on beaten roads lined with livestock and lushness.

We parked at look-offs and took photos of each other, proving our great bravery of RIDING A MOTORCYCLE IN THAILAND. It was a day of adventure and achievement. Something I didn't know was on my bucket list until the gentle wind flowed through my ocean waved hair.

As the end of the day neared, we were feeling pretty Hells Angels and mutually decided we'd take it up a notch. "I want to go fast," I shared with Mike, my eyes filled with rebellion and excitement. We agreed I would ride in front of Mike and set the pace. Travelling at what was surely jet speed, my blood turned to Red Bull. My heart pumped the caffeinated liquid through my body, my mind dizzy with laughter and bad-assery. We were motocross in the jungle. Champions of our sport. We were *Zen and the Art of Motorcycle Maintenance* meets Evel Knievel. Nothing could stop us.

As we conspired our gang colours and sleeve tattoos (that we would sit through in one session), the sun started to set and we neared the road back to our hotel. We were a force to be reckoned with. Martial law had nothing on us. We owned this town and could escape any threat on our trusty metal stallions.

I heard the roar of an engine coming up behind me. Mike must be making a move, proving his bravery and skill to ride side by side down the dusty roads, exactly down the yellow line. We would be two abreast arriving back in Pai, the lazy-hippie town that had surely been warned of the bike gang soon to arrive in their ordinarily peaceful streets.

I did a shoulder check to my left and was startled by the collection of faces. In an instant, another bike, similar to mine, passed me. There were so many people on it I could hardly take count, especially at the warp speed I thought we were moving.

It was a family reunion on a moped.

Driving this family was a tiny Thai girl, no more than nine, who had to stand upright on the bike to see over the handlebars. She weighed less than my helmet, and I believe was softly humming the nursery rhyme she had learned from her second-grade teacher that day at school. On the seat and rear fender sat—and stood—the entire rest of her bloodline. Parents, siblings, great aunts that they had met just once at a funeral, and newborn babies, breastfeeding and drooling. They all piled like a Jenga game atop a moped the size of a rocking horse, defying the rules of physics. Our egos shattered.

To drive in Canada the following rules must be obeyed to operate a vehicle: First, when you turn 16, you take a written driving test to evaluate your understanding of road signs, parking, and speed limits. If you pass *that* test, you're given a learner's permit, allowing you to drive between specific hours under the supervision of a more experienced driver. After three months of this apprenticeship, your training wheels are removed and your hard-plastic licence is upgraded from a Class 7 to a Class 5 after yet *another* test, finally proving your capability of driving safely on the roads.

But.

Before you can drive, you need a vehicle, of course. This vehicle must be purchased, registered, safety inspected, and insured before you are legally permitted to take it on the road. All of these tasks cost money. You have to outfit your vehicle with a safety inspection sticker in the window and a licence plate (with relevant registration stickers) on the back. Proof of insurance must be carried with you at all times, subject to a fine should you be caught without your paperwork. Once all of these details have been sorted, the "rules of the road" are applied. Speed limits are posted on massive signs, constantly reminding us of our menace and mortality. If you drive faster or slower than these speeds, you can be fined. You must use a signal light when turning or passing, you must shoulder check when veering right or left, you must wear a seat belt at all times, you must parallel park between 12 and 18 inches from the curb, you must turn your front wheels towards the curb when parking on a hill, you must engage your emergency brake when parking on a hill, you must park between the painted lines in a parking lot because someone took time to paint them. You must adhere to three-way stops, you must have no cracks in your windshield, you must have winter tires when the season changes, and you must have both headlights working at all times.

In Thailand, an entire baseball team could make it to practice on a single motorcycle they scored from Uncle Dwayne's scrapyard with siphoned gas and an oil leak. Whoever was at fault in an accident might have left with one fewer chickens or a black eye and the issue was settled. They parked where they wanted, when they wanted, and paid nothing for it. They could do this at nine or 90 years old, so long as they wanted to.

I wondered if my moment of biker babedom was less about speed and more about sovereignty. I wondered why Canada, one of the freest nations in the world, had laws so plentiful that something as common as driving had become available only to the restricted and privileged few. I wondered who had taught the nine-year-old girl to drive. I wondered if she even considered things like danger and road rage. I wondered who had it right.

As the family disappeared in the distance, so did my need for speed. I felt accomplished having improved our riding skills in just a single outing and that we would be returning the mopeds with no more scars than how we had started. Our bike gang of two had broader shoulders and confident smirks. My attention turned to the setting sun, and the figure of our hotel in the near distance.

"WHAT YOU NEED IS CASHMERE SUIT":

Scams and Stuff

On our first day in Thailand, we couldn't have stood out more. Our skin was glowing white. If you looked directly at us for more than four seconds, you'd go blind. At the very least develop cataracts. We were both sweating like we were on mile 26 of a marathon. It was sauna-like, by far the hottest place I'd ever been. My face was still randomly bleeding too. I'd be in the middle of a conversation and suddenly taste the blood running into my mouth. It was nice to know that the disgusted looks on people's faces were from my zombie-like appearance and not just my general repugnance. I had no idea what time it was, what day it was, or if I was even really alive. I thought it could be heaven. It was warm, food was cheap, and I felt like Shaq must feel in a room full of horse jockeys. If it was heaven, I guess it was as good a place as any.

> **TRAVEL TIP:** *Every city we're in we discover the majority of it by walking around. It's cheap, helps burn off the beer and doughnut calories, and you always stumble upon hidden gems you wouldn't otherwise. Shops, museums, restaurants, characters, etc. We tell people what we did and they never believe us. If you walk 10 hours a day, it's possible.*

We're used to walking all day when discovering a new city, but slobbering around in the heat of Bangkok after surviving a brain explosion, we decided to take it slow. We'd check out what was nearby and permitted for sweaty, dizzy, and bleeding tourists. This was precisely when we discovered two pivotal things that would be of major significance for the next month: 1) 7-Eleven and its ice-cold, air-conditioned inside that would serve as a body temperature regulating necessity, and 2) The Taylor Swift ice cream bar. She had a concert coming up that month in Bangkok and with a purchase of the T-Swift ice cream bar, you could win tickets to the show. My criteria for buying cold desserts is that they first be delicious, and second, the packaging must contain images of a tall blonde girl. We ate so many in Thailand that, with the presumed portion of Taylor's DNA in each snack, I started to know the words to her whole catalogue without having ever listened to a song. In the end her concert was cancelled due to the martial law, but I feel like a piece of Taylor now resides in me forever.

We found a park close to our hotel, picked up some T-Swift ice cream bars, and decided to attempt drying our armpits there. When we walked through the gate of the park, I saw a six-foot lizard clinging to a tree.

A giant, real-life lizard.

"Oh my God, a lizard!" I yelled. "What are the chances of that?!" On day one, in the very first park we entered, on the very first tree we looked at, there was a giant lizard. I held Kristen's hand. Our luck was almost implausible. I started to look around. As I focused in, as I sunk into my surroundings and forgot about the 30 hour travel day, the fatigue and the jet lag, and truly let my senses focus in, I realized there were lizards all around us. Everywhere I looked there was a giant demon lizard bigger than the last. Baby ones ran around our feet. Lizards clung to palm trees, their bugged out eyes darting around. Lizards went about their daily routines doing lizardy things in their lizard wonderland. I didn't know it at the time, but scaly, four-legged reptiles would come into play more often than not during that trip.

Earlier that day I found a map of the city at the hotel. The things I'm best at in life are finding decent clothes at used clothing stores, kicking extremely high objects, and figuring out a map in a new city. I need about an hour to get my bearings, figure out directions, link a few landmarks, and I'm good to go. We sat in the park, naming the lizards (Estaban, Steve

Buscemi and Sharon were our favourites) and I did my mental work to get accustomed to the massive city.

And we ventured out.

Bangkok is a loud, massive, and bustling city overflowing with vibrancy, colourful people, and a surplus of smells. I've never been somewhere that I noticed so many scents. Food, piss, garbage, flowers, cologne, death, and life filled the streets with every step. We trekked through the city letting the feeling of newness fill us up. With martial law in effect, the streets were lined with soldiers and their massive machine guns. After the initial shock wore off, we realized they were mainly just young kids fresh out of boot camp who were less threatening than a bowl of M&Ms. People were getting pictures with them and they'd even let a pretty girl hold the gun if she smiled the right way.

Not 30 minutes into our wandering, a police officer approached us. I was nervous since Thai prisons are known around the world as being fairly rapey and stabby and the glow on my skin alone was probably enough for a three to five year sentence.

"Where you from?" he asked, smiling all the while.

Canada we told him.

"Oh, Canada! I love Canada! What part, Toronto or Vancouver?"

When we realized that we weren't going to get arrested for endangering the retinas of the general public, we became excited. This man was just curious. This man of the law was genuinely interested in who we were.

"Well . . . it's a little further east than Toronto, a place called Nova Scotia."

"Oh Winnipeg!"

"That's pretty much it!"

"How you very like Thailand?"

"Well, we just got here . . . it's beautiful though."

He looked me up and down, my body sweating profusely, possibly about to take a heart attack or just generally erupt from my rising body heat.

"Big Guy . . . what you need is cashmere suit!"

I was confused. Me? A cashmere suit? His assessment of me—six foot four, 225-pound mass of irrepressible disgusting drip, wearing a tank top, swim shorts, flip-flops, and sweating so much that it looked like there was a hose attached to the top of my head perpetually pouring over my body—was that I needed MORE clothes. And a thick, tightly woven, heavy fabric like cashmere at that! The second we landed in Thailand, my body decided that it would sweat forever more. Every second. And not just a cute little sheath on the forehead like when you change a light-bulb up really high and your girlfriend thinks you're sweet and handy, I'm talking full on balls to the wall hyperventilating military hill sprint drip. My elbow was sweating. I looked like I was crying constantly.

I thought maybe I misheard him, that the combination of a time change, my brain bursting on the plane and the heat was getting to me.

"Uhhh . . . we're just trying to find the Emerald Buddha now," I said, assuming the suit comment was a figment of my imagination. Maybe his English teacher taught him the wrong word. Maybe cashmere suit meant "pad thai" or "young prostitute."

"Oh what you need to do is take tuk-tuk ride. They take you everywhere!"

"A tuk-tuk?"

"Oh yes . . . Look here come one now!"

A small, three-wheeled cart of sorts pulled up at this exact time. I looked at Kristen. The moment we needed a ride, it happened. While travelling, you're often faced with an array of questions and options. Sometimes, when the choice is made for you, you just have to follow it. The police officer encouraged us to get in. We walked towards the small vehicle and asked if he could take us to the Emerald Buddha.

"Oh, yes, yes . . . I take you there! Fifty baht."

Fifty baht is basically the equivalent to two bucks. If it cost us less than a toonie, it was a deal we couldn't pass up. The friendly police officer waved as we got in and jetted off.

We drove on, through the red-light district, past the prostitutes and their suitors, the smell of debauchery in the air, and a city pulsating with the heartbeat of mankind's eternal energy. I held Kristen's hand. Our journey was beginning. We were in Bangkok, in the thick of it all. This is what travel was all about—whizzing through something entirely new while your senses overload to take it all in.

We flew through the crowded streets of the city. The drivers there have no fear. I don't even think they have brakes. They just go full speed, millimetres beside a million others doing the same. There are no seatbelts, no rules at all it seems. But no one ever loses their temper. They just calmly proceed through the insanity.

We had looked up the Emerald Buddha at some point before and wanted to check it out. It's a massive, beautiful Buddhist temple that's the most sacred in all of Thailand. It's said that it watches over the Thai nation as a protector and source of divine power.

The tuk-tuk stopped in front of a small Thai temple that looked identical to about 50 we had already passed along the way.

"This better than Emerald Buddha!" the driver said.

This driver knew the city so well, he knew the hidden gems and the places that the tourists—the people like us—don't often get to see. If the Emerald Buddha was known worldwide as a magnificent and sacred place and this spot was *better*, I couldn't imagine what lay inside.

The driver told us he would wait and we went inside. It was a small temple with a lone monk sitting on the floor. He was bald and wearing an orange robe. He wasn't meditating, just sitting there smiling at us.

"Take seat!" he implored.

Wow, an actual Buddhist monk was inviting us into his place of worship! This was amazing. This was a story we'd tell years from now. Maybe just talking to him would enlighten us. Maybe we'd come out of this magical temple with all the answers we had ever pined for.

We took off our shoes and sat down on the floor in front of him, making sure to keep our feet pointed away from the altar.

> **TRAVEL TIP:** *If you're going somewhere with cultural differences that may vary from your usual life, try to look them up beforehand. In doing this, we had learned that in a Buddhist temple you never face your feet towards the altar; it's considered disrespectful.*

"Where you from?" he asked.

"Canada," we told him in unison, both of us excited.

"Oh! Toronto or Vancouver?

"Actually . . . it's on the East coast in Nova Scotia."

"Oh Montreal!"

At least he was closer than the other guy.

"Me, Gary. I was professor at Cambridge University in England. Now I monk here. I am friends with Australian superstar Broderick Lloyd Jones!"

The man was an authentic genius. To be a professor at one of the world's most renowned collegiate institutions, you have to be in an elite percentage of human intelligence. I didn't know who Broderick Lloyd Jones was, but when you verbally refer to someone as a "superstar" they're instantly legitimized in my eyes. And he was his friend! I wondered if he was the Australian Brad Pitt? If he was a lady slayer like the real Brad. I wondered if Broderick Lloyd Jones and Gary got up to no good painting the town red and smooth-talking 10/10s to bring back to the temple?

"Wow . . ." was all I could say.

"You a very big guy," he said. "What you need is cashmere suit. Very warm, very comfortable."

At that exact moment in time, other than being impressed that Gary knew B. L. J. in real life, all I wanted was to be naked and dipped in a vat of glacial ice from the farthest reaches of the north.

"I think I'm good, bud!" I said, pointing to my general state of perspiration. "I never really wore a suit in my life and it's the last thing on my mind. A tank top, shorts and flip-flops is *by far* the most I could wear without spontaneously combusting into a heap of sludge on the floor."

"Big guy with a big suit," he said. "Cashmere, best in Thailand. If someone offers to take you to suit store, you go with them."

We sat in the temple and tried to meditate. Every few minutes Gary would interrupt us with a fact about how good the suits were or tell a brief anecdote about his and Broderick Lloyd Jones' adventures in the world abroad.

"Tough to meditate with this goddamn monk here," I whispered to Kristen, maybe the first time the sentence uttered in the history of the universe.

We left the temple and got back to the tuk-tuk. The driver sat there like it was the last place he wanted to be, even though he was the one who suggested we go there.

"Emerald Buddha!" I told him!

"Yes, yes!"

We started to drive. As we were buzzing along, finally on our way to the sacred temple, the driver handed us a brochure on suits. When I lifted my head up to give a "What the hell is this?" kind of comment, we had already pulled over in front of a suit store.

"Go in!" he said.

"No, man . . . I don't want a suit at all. It's the last thing I want. Just take us to the Emerald Buddha!"

Four other Thai men came outside and surrounded the tuk-tuk.

"Very good suits in here . . . Cashmere for Big Guy!" one of them said.

I realized at this point the intricacies of the scam they were putting us through. The police officer who stopped us on the street was not an actual police officer. He was just an idiot who, like other idiots I know, probably answered true and false to short answer questions on a Grade 10 science test (Question: Explain the process of photosynthesis. Answer: True). He was hired by a group of other idiots to wear a fake costume and find naïve tourists on their first day in Bangkok. Our glowing white skin, confused moronic looks on our faces, and the map in my hands made us easy targets. He asked where we were from to try and create some kind of familiarity. Each idiot memorized two cities from all the countries where people typically travel from. They pose as trustworthy professions: cops, teachers, doctors, etc. The tuk-tuk driver was working with the cop. "Gary," the learned professor from Cambridge was a plant. His real name was probably Sereemongkonpol or Bhadajarabhakinai. He likely learned English from Van Damme movies and got blackout drunk at least once a week. I used to think I was fairly smart. I read, have an appetite for continuous learning and try to soak in everything I can about the human experience. I was duped by a man with broken English who said he was a professor at one of the world's top post secondary institutions and introduced himself with "Me, Gary."

It was all about the suit.

The fucking cashmere suit.

The whole point was to get us to this store and try to get us to buy something. I wanted the opposite of a suit. I wanted a banana hammock Speedo I could walk around in and let my sweat drip off freely.

We were surrounded by four men. I thought maybe the best bet was to just walk away, to find a piece of dog shit somewhere, come back and light it on fire in a paper bag at the entrance to the store. But I didn't know where we were. I didn't have my bearings or know what would happen if we just up and left. I figured the best option was to go inside and at least entertain them. We'd look around for a bit and then just get the hell out. The tuk-tuk driver could take us somewhere I could at least pinpoint on a map.

We went inside. They were all smiling and friendly, but something was definitely off. They tried to separate us; take Kristen one way and me the other. I grabbed Kristen by the arm and shook my head. I probably outweighed each of them by a hundred pounds. I figured if it came to it, I could crush at least two of their skulls and get Kristen out before everything went to hell. We walked around and tried to appear calm. After a few minutes, I said we had to get going. They had people trying to measure me. "Best suits in Thailand!" they explained, their hands all over my body. I gave one guy a moderately-friendly-used-to-play-hockey-when-I-was-younger Canadian bodycheck and pushed him to the side. I took Kristen's hand and we walked down the stairs and outside. The driver was there and surprised to see us out that quick and without a suit.

"No suit for Big Guy?"

"Just take us to the Emerald Buddha, bud."

He drove for about 20 minutes and dropped us off. We were probably closer to Canada than we were to the Emerald Buddha.

It was starting to get dark and we were lost in a massive city.

"What we'll do when we get back is go out for a real nice supper," I said.

"That sounds lovely," Kristen said as I stared at the map and tried not to show any panic.

"We'll get dressed up real good . . . I'll put on a suit . . . oh wait . . . If only . . . ."

She punched me in the arm and we both started to laugh.

ART GALLERIES GONE RIGHT:
The Things You Find

New York:

Every visit to New York City offers a memorable moment: the dive bar with hundreds of bras hanging from the ceiling, roaming around Times Square drinking Hudson Rivers (a custom cocktail we invented that includes coconut water, pineapple juice, and blackberry brandy), receiving complementary Chi Gong energy work in Central Park, and then there was that time that Mike broke the strap on his flip-flop and had to walk 20 city blocks with one foot bare before finding a flea market where he bought a stinky $4 pair of used Nikes to tide him over. There always seems to be room for the unknown. Despite our planning, something unexpected IS part of the New York experience.

On this particular trip, we were staying in the Chelsea District, one of our favourite neighbourhoods. It was littered with art galleries and eccentrics, where anonymity and glitz make eye contact on the Highline, where history asks the future out for cocktails (likely Hudson Rivers), and where two unlikely, small-town Canadians were invited to a private art tour of one of China's most renowned artist's collections in the wee hours of a Thursday morning.

The blackened sidewalks held the remnants of last nights' rain and risky behaviours. I was on a hunt for coffee, not quite ready for anything else until properly caffeinated. On route to the Chelsea Market, we were intercepted by a seven-foot man, wearing a suit and special agent sunglasses. It was 8 a.m. He opened the door to what looked like an unmarked warehouse from the outside and gestured for us to enter.

Mike and I exchanged a quick glance, nonverbally questioning what we should do. Like so many times before this, we said yes to the unknown. It would prove to be one of the most impressive art exhibits we had ever seen.

There aren't many things I'm in the mood for before my multiple morning coffees, but browsing international art galleries seemed a worthy exception. I've been an artist for a number of years, making abstract art and refurbishing vintage furniture with my own fabrics and paints. Being introduced to new forms, colours, shapes, and stories makes me a better artist and inspired creator. When I return to my studio after travelling, I'm guaranteed to have visions though fresh eyes. If a random giant wanted to offer me a private viewing in the art capital of the world at the ass crack of dawn, caffeine could wait.

Room after room, we were presented with intricate wall murals, nuanced with custom mixed colours and shapes. Elephant-sized sculptures were suspended from high ceilings, glimmering under the overhead lights. Behind-the-scenes video footage revealed teams of apprentice artists constructing the artwork, every piece carefully placed and polished. Golden dragons and cartoon-like characters popped off canvases and rose from the earth. Secret Service-like men were lurking in every corner as we meandered carefully through spaces. We did not look like art dealers or wealthy collectors. We looked like who we truly were: two small-town nobodies in need of coffee, but somehow found ourselves as the only two people on a private tour with artwork priced in the millions.

I grabbed a brochure as we were leaving. If Takashi Murakami invited me to collaborate, I would have a reference of his work at my fingertips. He's also worked with Kanye West, Louis Vuitton, and Billy Eilish, so it seemed reasonable that he would reach out to a middle-aged artist from rural Nova Scotia any day now. He sold a sculpture in 2008 for $15.2 million. The piece, *My Lonesome Cowboy*, was an anime-inspired sculpture of a masturbating boy whose semen stream forms a lasso. This was an encouraging lesson in artistic liberty, creative vision, and that sex and cowboys are timeless. The opportunity set the tone for the day by reminding us that adventure has no boundaries. Adventure does not discriminate against wealth and appearance. Adventure is often, just behind an unassuming warehouse door, held open by a giant in a freshly-pressed suit.

Vienna:

It even sounds romantic: "Vienna." When you imagine this historic city you can't help but think of ornate architecture, hats with hand-sewn lace, and shoulder pads affixed with taxidermy birds. And of course, classical art. We make a point of seeking out the cultural hubs in the places we visit. These communities reliably offer accepting smiles, forward-thinking conversation and, typically, exceptional coffee and cuisine. We discovered "sissy water" in Vienna. We're not entirely sure this is the pronunciation, or really even close to what water mixed with mint leaves, sliced lemon, and cucumber pieces was called, but we've stuck with sissy water ever since and it tastes delicious regardless of what we name it.

> **TRAVEL TIP:** *Take some time to research what neighbourhood you want to stay in. It doesn't have to necessarily be in proximity to the main attractions. You can find ways to get to those. Rather, focus on staying in a place with like-minded people, where you feel at home and at ease.*

We also (unintentionally) discovered the art gallery of Elena Mildred. Another private tour of a foreign gallery started with our two curious faces peering into a space we believed to be empty or abandoned. Just steps off the cobblestone sidewalk, Burggasse 21 was a curious venue inviting our attention. We could see provocative canvases covered in red painted lips and other erotic body parts. There were boxes and papers on the floor as though someone was either mid-project or had left in haste. The gallery was near our hotel, so we had walked by it two or three times already, each time my senses allured by the gallery's obscurities.

On this particular afternoon, with my face once again pressed on the windows of what I believed to be an unopened gallery, a second face met mine on the other side of the glass. Startled by the sudden appearance of a woman with blunt-cut bangs and cat-eye glasses, I felt like I had been caught in a misunderstood peeping-Tom act. It was Elena Mildred. Her sharp features softened as she opened the door a crack and asked if we'd like to come in. I believe I lunged myself into the space without saying yes and without confirming if Mike was coming with me. Sometimes with art, you're no longer in charge. Paintings can cast a spell on your imagination and sing sweet lullabies until they've mesmerized your corneas and cranium.

Elena pegged us as "poor students."

"I assume you're visiting on a student visa?" she concluded, looking up and down at our tattered travel clothes. We nodded our heads sheepishly, aware of the raspberry jam from the morning's breakfast still crusted at the corners of our mouths. I didn't care. We played along and as a result, were given the VIP pity-party tour of her private collection. Ms. Mildred's works were showcased in a massive labyrinth of chambers in the basement of the building. We wandered throughout the various brick-walled rooms —painted all white—filled with blotches of colour on canvas that looked like how ice cream might taste if you were on LSD.

Her latest works "Live Drive" used skateboards as her paintbrush; swirls of paint, transferred through the tricks of the wheels onto the white-washed fabrics. The abstract technique reminded me of my own artwork and I thought about how I might integrate new tools and textures into a fresh collection. Surrounded by vibrant palettes and European history made my fingers tingle in anticipation of unwrapping a blank canvas.

Elena's Russian accent bounced around the rooms as she patiently described her process and partnership with the "skater" community. I was reminded of the first time I ever rode a skateboard. On my second day living in Vancouver, at 18, and an entire country away from my family and friends, "I dropped into a bowl" and fractured my wrist skateboarding with a stoned hippie whose dreadlocks smelled like ham and wool socks. I wondered if Elena had ever broken her leg doing a 360 toe flip.

I was in awe of the abstract execution Elena showed and even more so with her willingness to entertain a couple of straggler-students who were curious about art. Exposure to how other artists push their boundaries and marry mediums is always energizing. Travelling is about more than being on vacation. For artists like us, it's research, collaboration, inspiration, and fire for the projects we'll start when we get back to our studios.

New Orleans:

Mike and I stick together on most of our outings when we're abroad. It's partly for safety reasons, but more so because we *want* to be doing the same things. There have been a few exceptions to this rule: the time that Mike took a Thai boxing lesson in 47-degree heat (I got a massage); the time that Mike got us a bag of duck feet for supper while warding off a gang (I slept at the hotel); and the time that Mike simply wandered ahead in New Orleans while I went shoe shopping.

B.E.E Galleries is located in the French Quarter and hosts up to 15 resident artists at a time. The walls are high and rooms are spacious. Ranging from resin figurines to pop-art to landscapes, the gallery has a down-to-earth energy where you don't feel like clearing your throat or scuffing your shoe will create an invasive shock wave of sound throughout the entire city. I've never understood why art galleries enforce a sleeping baby's silence. I much prefer a vibrant, musical, open space where I can laugh and talk and interact with the artwork.

When I gradually worked my way from shop to shop, looking to catch up with Mike who had run (literally) ahead while I admired footwear, I was delighted to find him at a gallery. He was near the back, chatting with a curator when I entered. There were probably a thousand works of art in this space. With a vast collection of artists and styles, it was hard to know where to begin. But like a magnetic force had been installed between my pupils and the paint, I walked directly up to a 24- by 36-inch masterpiece that was heavy with girthy globs of colour. It hung higher than my height; I looked upwards upon the shining, protruding flowers and swirling acrylic skies in the background. There was something about this painting, more than all of the others, including the famous Martin LaBordes that graced the walls opposite.

"I love this painting," I said to Mike, who was now standing behind me, my eyes still fixated on the plumpy palette.

"I was just telling the sales guy over there that this one was MY favourite!" he replied, amazement in his voice.

Of all the creations under one roof, we separately gravitated towards the exact same painting.

It was completely out of our price range, it was a ridiculous souvenir, it would be cumbersome to ship it all the way to Nova Scotia, it was not a responsible item to acquire when we needed so many other things.

And today, *Spring Evening* painted by Ed Edwards, a former military soldier who was seeking colour amidst his time served abroad, surrounded by only sand, proudly hangs in our living room.

KOKO'S MASTERPIECE:
Love and Shit

In terms of the worst travel shit *I* ever had, it's fairly hard to choose. The thing about travelling is that a good third of it is just horrific shitting disasters. And that's fine. You can only talk about getting a tan, sunsets, and "had to be there moments" to your friends for so long. Eventually, the real stories come out—the shit stories. That's what everyone wants to hear. Yeah, the food was good and all . . . but did you have to shit in a tub? Did you get chased down an alley by a gang who you fought off with diarrhea?

For me, I think I have to go with the episode at the elephant reserve in Thailand. We rode a cute elephant named Moola who we told ourselves was treated well and had lots of room to run around. At night they gave her an endless bucket of peanuts and all the animals got together to dance and tell each other how much they loved each other.

Either way, it sure as hell was fun to ride on top of a giant animal and put all your trust into her. After our ride, Moola's younger buds were doing an art show. I didn't know it myself, but elephants are phenomenal artists. They grab that brush with their trunk and go to town, every piece a Van Gogh-like triumph.

At least that's what I remember. This was at the point when the "Thai Gurgles" started to kick in. It doesn't take long for a traveller from small town Nova Scotia to know what this means. By day two in Bangkok, the concept of "using the bathroom" had turned to "erupt like the world is ending and the source of destruction lies at your anus."

When the Thai Gurgles started, I nodded to Kristen and she knew. There's a beautiful thing about getting to know someone on that deeper level. You can communicate a whole novel with a quick glance. Things you'd never say or do early on become commonplace. This trip brought us closer together on a level I'd never experienced before then. There's only so much you can learn about someone when you're dressed up and talking over a candle-lit dinner drinking martinis. You either fall apart or bond and become inseparable when you're sharing a small room and have only eaten curry for a month.

Koko may have been creating the next *Mona Lisa*, but I was on a mission to the nearest bathroom. I bolted out as the crowd cheered in awe. Thankfully the toilet was around the corner. There were six "stalls" and I went into the last one, assuming it to be the least used. There was a hole in the ground about as round as a grapefruit. No seat. No handles. Just a small hole and the need for extreme accuracy. I was never one to be able to bend my knees. I played sports my whole life, could jump pretty high, and run for miles, but I could never really bend my knees. Even when I was in little league baseball, I couldn't play catcher because I couldn't get into that position—at eight years old. At 32, my legs might as well have just been solid two by fours.

I dropped my shorts and bent the two inches my knees would allow. With the Thai Gurgles there's not a whole lot of planning that happens. You drop your shorts and the bomb goes off. There was a large amount of precision, angles, geometry, and physics needed to pull this off accurately. What happened was the exact opposite of that. If I was told that when I got into that stall my sole purpose was to not allow ONE DROP to enter that hole, I would have emerged a king of grand proportions.

The saga of the Titanic is often used as a metaphor for disastrous failure. What happened in that sixth stall on a hot day in Thailand at the elephant reserve while Koko painted her masterpiece was nothing short of a definitive tragedy far surpassing the fateful voyage of the infamous ship. The explosion shot like an unmanned firehose everywhere I didn't want it to go. My legs were covered, my shorts covered, my feet covered. Not a single drop made it into that hole.

I stood there, bent over two inches and thought that this was as bad as it could get. This was my rock bottom. I was covered in shit, pouring sweat, and the nearest toilet paper was a three-hour bus ride away. In the surging swirl of life and its ups and downs, I was on a very down part of it all. And then I heard footsteps. A lone man softly singing to himself came into the bathroom. There was water running. He opened a door to a stall. I heard the sound of splashing. He was cleaning the stalls. And by cleaning the stalls, this meant that he went into stall number one and threw buckets of water onto the floor so it washed the shit and piss off the ground. That elixir ran down the sloped ground and continued to "clean" the floors of stalls one through five till it got to six—where I was—and emptied out of a hole in the wall beside me. I could hear the water coming but there was nothing I could do. I was still using 100 per cent of my brain power to figure out how to get the shit off my body. If Heidi Klum walked by and told me to come with her I would just shake my head, "figuring out shit situation." I heard the water coming but it was inevitable.

And then it hit me.

The swirl of water and shit and piss and whatever else from stalls one through five ran over my feet. I could see chunks of this, chunks of that. My feet were being covered in the washout of a thousand turds and mishaps.

I didn't cry, but I started to fake sob. That's basically crying, I suppose. As I watched the shit water wash over my feet, a lizard fell from the roof and onto my shoulder.

A. Fucking. Lizard.

I was covered in my own shit, had a tsunami of other people's on my feet and now had a lizard to deal with.

I closed my eyes and wondered how Koko's painting ended up. Did he create his magnum opus? Was I missing out on the birth of his masterpiece?

I knew that getting back to a position where I could, at the very least, be compared favourably to a trash can was a multi-step process. My first order of business was to get my new friend off me. He wasn't big, but any size lizard is still a fucking lizard. I started to wiggle. I've never been possessed, but assume that the movements I made were similar to those when a spirit is leaving one's body. I wiggled for all I was worth. It wasn't quite dancing, but similar to a hippie at Burning Man takes ALL THE DRUGS type of shuffle.

When I opened my eyes, the lizard was gone. I couldn't see it anywhere so there's a fair chance that the only thing that got into the hole that day was poor little baby Godzilla.

Next, I had to get some level of the shit off me. I'd be happy with 70 per cent, but knew anything close to 50 per cent would be respectable. I took my shorts off and walked out of the stall. My bottom half was bare and hanging freely, but I didn't care. It's hard to really care about anything in that situation, and a dangling penis in public was not on the list.

I had heard the man running water so knew there was a tap somewhere nearby. I scoured every inch of the wall until I found it. It was so low to the floor it might as well have just come out of the ground. There was at most, a foot of space to get my naked body under. I was already so far into the not giving a fuck stage, I just laid down on the ground under the tap and rolled around with the water flowing, my dong flopping around and people walking in trying with all their available strength to avoid eye contact with me.

I got up, ran the water over my clothes and rung them out. I was soaked and pathetic but more or less clean. I got dressed and walked back to the show, hoping to catch a glimpse of Koko's masterpiece.

NIGHT CRAWLERS:

Love Story #3

A second date is similar to a first date: outfit planning, activity preparation, being nervous, being excited, and being comforted by the fact that both parties hadn't been so thrown off by the terrible-teen-sex-cult-indie-film-failure and bullet-hard-charred-to-hell muffins that a second date was even happening.

It was a rainy day and Mike had planned to come over to my apartment again. He didn't have a place of his own at the time. My friends started teasing me that I was dating a homeless guy. I didn't see it that way but suppose by definition they were right. My mildewy one-bedroom basement apartment with angry upstairs neighbours didn't seem like much to brag about either. With both of us having grown up in moderately poor, rural Nova Scotia families, I was just happy to have cereal in the cupboard and some third-hand furniture to sit on. My friends had also dubbed Michael Stephen Ryan as MSR, later flipped to RSM for "Rat-Sword-Man" when I told them about the time he chopped off a rat's tail with a sword.

I opted for a more casual outfit this time around. Recognizing RSM had worn surfer shorts and a banana T-shirt last time, I felt much less pressure about my wardrobe selection. It was nice, actually. I'm sure lots of women would have been turned off, not being picked up in a nice car, en route to a dinner at a place where you couldn't really hear each other and the napkins cost more than my bedsheets. But I wasn't one of those women. I liked that there wasn't enormous pressure to impress one another. Or maybe there *was* and we had just failed miserably at this dating thing we were both new to. Either way, I felt like the faded ripped jeans and hoodie I selected, both second-hand finds, would be suitable.

My confidence in this decision rose when Mike showed up for date number two wearing his blue printed surfer shorts and his Dole banana T-shirt.

Again.

His repeat outfit was particularly funny to me because a favourite story of my parents' early years is about their first and second dates. Ma had bought a new dress and earrings for their first date. Dad showed up in a corduroy buffalo suit. A corduroy buffalo suit is exactly what it sounds like: a brownish colour base fabric, covered with images of charging buffalos, repeated over and over on the soft, ridged pants and sports coat. The suit was not new. But it was sweet in that Dad obviously felt it was a worthy date outfit. So much so, he wore it *again* on their second date. A couple of things going on here: how is it possible that this had happened on my parents' first two dates and was now happening on mine? What are the odds of two women *liking* that? Was this a "thing" that I shared with my mother in terms of the qualities we found attractive in men? And secondly, how was it that a buffalo suit and a banana shirt were the choices that these men were so confident in, they, without question, went for it twice in a row? The joke is really on us. I might make fun of their fashion choices, but these guys clearly knew what their end game was. We married them, after all.

I didn't comment on the banana shirt, though I did tell Mike I liked his jacket—a royal blue, snap-front jacket with yellow stripes and a patch that said "Legion 1987" on the front and someone else's name embroidered on the sleeve.

"Have you ever gone looking for night crawlers?" Mike asked. He had decided he was going to pick the activity this date. I felt he was getting off relatively easy as anything would be better than the movie night I tortured us with last time.

"Umm, I don't think so," I said. Had I? What the hell was a night crawler? Was it the name of a biker gang, or a hipster band? Was it like being a "Dead Head"? Groupie slang for pursuing the band, The Night

Crawlers, as they toured around secret venues and only the cool kids knew the password to get past the bouncers?

"You know, those giant worms? They're the best after the rain."

Night crawlers. Those giant, snake-sized worms that are born out of puddles and scary dreams. Those brown, sludgy, slimy piles of goo that take your breath away in disgust. They're slime in motion and if you step on one, you slide like a banana peel would down a water slide. I had only seen them once and had never actively pursued finding them. I'm certain that goes without saying. One time when I was a kid, I went digging for clams with my parents at a cottage we had rented. I accidentally dug up a *Tremors*-meets-anaconda-like demon from the depths of the sand, a "night crawler," my father had called it. For the first time in 20 years, I was reminded these creatures exist.

Mike somehow thought that taking a girl to look for giant slime monsters was a good idea. Maybe it was. Somehow, the unusual suggestion, paired with the recycled banana shirt was peaking my interest in a rapid way. This guy had exactly zero inhibitions and I appreciated that his date idea, albeit the weirdest date of all time, was creatively genius.

Hunting for night crawlers ended up being both memorable and freeing. We walked around my neighbourhood, the sun down and the sidewalks glimmering wet with that after-rain sheen. Every block or so we'd point out a giant eel-sized worm on the ground, glistening under the beam of our flashlight. We compared sizes and features to others we had seen on the walk. We gave some of them names and jumped over others if they were larger than a baby beaver. The date was more about walking and talking, adventuring together and inserting a purpose to keep it light and funny. This would set the tone for how we communicated and felt around each other in years to come. It would always be fun, adventurous, and interesting. There would always be creativity between us and odd suggestions that led to unexpected discoveries.

Night crawler hunting will not show up in a dating advice column. It will never be the idea suggested by your friends, family, co-workers, therapist or iconic figure. No one in the history of dating has ever gone night crawler hunting on their second (or any) date. Ever. In the strangest way, it's part of what set us apart from the rest. It's what made Mike "the one."

CLARENCE HOT:

Love Story #4

Kristen grew up in a small town called Clarence. When she first told me where she was from I laughed. I didn't mean to, but really, it was hard not to. It's a *place* called Clarence. Not your alcoholic great uncle who makes moonshine to sell to fishermen, not the man who fixes TVs for a living but only knows how to work on Zeniths, and not the redneck with onion breath who made you do shots before you sang and didn't tell you it was hot-sauce and tequila. It was a place. And it was her home.

The first time I went there was after a weekend of camping at a music festival. We drove along the shore with the windows down and the cool breeze of the Atlantic filling our lungs. We were exhausted but had the energy you get after a weekend being exactly what you need it to be. Our feet were sore and muddy from dancing for hours straight. It was the first time we ever did that together and it felt nice.

When we got to Clarence, I realized it wasn't so much a town as it was just a road with farms spread along it periodically. There were no stores or even businesses in general. Just cows and the smell of fertilizer. Kristen's house was the first place built in Clarence, where the first settlers lived. One previous owner died having a shit in the outhouse. I thought that was pretty neat.

I had met Kristen's parents once before. Her mom was sweet and her dad liked to joke around about everything. I liked them both.

Everyone in Kristen's family is short. She's five two and three-quarters. Her mom was about the same and her dad slightly taller. Her house is over 200 years old, back when people were even shorter. When I walked in I was like an ogre. It seemed like everywhere I went there was something at the exact right height to hit my head on. Light fixtures, door frames, the basement ceiling . . . basically every available inanimate object was fair game for my forehead.

Kristen's mom had made a fish chowder. I was starving. I was kind of hungover, but at the point where I could eat an entire horse and it would bring me back to 100 per cent.

She served each of us a bowl and sat down herself. It smelled so good. I could pick out the individual smells and the beautiful combination of seafood and vegetables. I took my first spoonful. It was piping hot. A mouth burner. "That was amazingly delicious but OBVIOUSLY too hot," I thought to myself. I figured that I'd put my spoon down, like everyone else would, converse for a brief amount of time and wait 10 or so minutes for it to cool down. When I looked up, Kristen's dad was already halfway through his bowl. Kristen and her mom were pounding it back like it was a nice, cool chocolate pudding. What was happening? What was wrong with these people? Was the inside of their mouths made up of some type of different and stronger flesh? Had people from Clarence developed an extra thick skin on the insides of their mouths?

I didn't know what to do. It was much too hot to eat, but they dug in like temperature had no impact on them. I didn't want to make it seem like either I was weak, or I didn't enjoy the meal. I put a spoonful into my mouth and tried to act like I wasn't swallowing molten lava. Her dad picked up the bowl and drank the last few drops. How was he done already? How did he consume that entire bowl of heat like an elephant?

I kept going. I couldn't appear fragile. This was important. It was the first time I'd been to their house and second time meeting them. I had to appear as though I had a strong or at least average mouth. Who would want their daughter dating a man with such weak mouth skin?

Her dad's spoon rattled in the bowl as he got up from the table to put it in the sink. Kristen and her Mom were halfway through and I had only consumed three spoonfuls.

I started to try to tell a story to make it look like the reason I wasn't eating was because my mouth was doing other things. As I talked and talked about golf courses and how I'd never seen the movie *Titanic*, the soup was cooling. The flames were dissipating, the fire easing. I tried to tie together my two unrelated topics and mentioned something about how I heard Leonardo DiCaprio was a good golfer. I lied but I had to. I didn't know if Leo ever golfed. But it didn't matter. Once that bowl hit even a moderately normal temperature I dove in headfirst. My mouth was already charred and mangled and would likely hurt for weeks, but I had to finish that soup.

I cleaned every drop and told Kristen's mom how good it was. I finished last out of the four of us, but at least I finished.

I wondered if it was some form of test. Was I served an extra-hot bowl to see how I'd respond? Were Kristen's parents psychopaths who wanted my mouth to blister in pain? I suppose everything is a form of test when you're meeting in-laws. They're obviously going to judge you, your actions and what their intuition says. Their observations were probably something along the lines of: "nice enough guy with a weak mouth who tells weird stories. Very tall with a fairly strong skull and forehead."

And I was happy with that. I wasn't perfect, but I wasn't Charles Manson. My mouth may have been weak, but my solid forehead made up for it to some degree.

Later, I asked Kristen about the chowder. She said that she didn't notice anything. I didn't know what that meant about her but it didn't matter. If her family were maniacs or another life-form from an advanced civilization with indestructible mouth innards, I didn't care. I was falling for her, whatever she was.

And now, when something is exceptionally hot, we have a name to refer to it by. Clarence Hot.

Thai Mom:
The Kindness of Others

In most countries, domestic travel is cheaper by bus than plane. Riding on a rusted-out tin can with a hole cut in the bottom for a bathroom and a piece of cloth thrown over a plastic bucket for toilet seats will surely save you a few bucks. Dozens of people pile in, always outnumbering available seats. They'll likely be accompanied by two or more chickens and five or more kids. The bus will be too hot, too loud, and not at all smooth on the roads. When it comes to blind corners on one-way streets, the trick is to lay on the horn and hope to hell an oncoming vehicle isn't doing the same at that very moment. These are the accepted road rules. We're not fancy and we're not squeamish, so bussing is the way we often go. That said, when we cost compared our transportation options in Thailand, for $60 you could spend 16 hours on said bus to travel from the southern beaches to the northern city of Chiang Mai. For $40 you could spend 90 minutes on a plane to cover the same distance. Who knew?

The airport was basic, but like all hub locations that host international travellers, we were graced with the gold standard of people watching. High traffic, multicultural, lots of turnover and for the most part, inhibitions are thrown out the door. I conclude that when there are that many strangers crammed into the same space, a feeling of such anonymity washes over, you might as well be completely alone. "No one will be watching *me*" you think to yourself. You're preoccupied with catching a connection or finding the loose gummy bears in your purse.

But trust me, we see you.

When we landed, we were less interested in people-watching and more interested in finding our rented hut. We were staying on the outskirts of Chiang Mai as our flight arrived in the evening and we wanted something nearby. The taxi dropped us off at the edge of a long driveway that led to a collection of thatched huts and a main house. I felt like we had stepped into the Seven Dwarfs dwellings and hoped that we were assigned "Sleepy's" hut for a restful night. A sweet, middle-aged Thai woman greeted us at the door of the main house, open-armed and smiling as though we were the most important people on earth. Her kindness was immediate as she gestured us into her home. Her English surpassed our Thai in the way a Rolls Royce surpasses rollerblades. We were grateful for her gentle presence and fresh treats she offered before we had even set down our backpacks. Mike and I both felt it. She was our Thai mom.

Mom guided us down a twisting path towards hut number seven, Sleepy's Hut, I intuitively knew. "Mom would see we got a good night's sleep," I thought to myself. She explained the intricacies, most of which I didn't pay attention to other than how the air conditioning worked. When you're provided directions on A/C in Thailand, you transform into a blood hound who has just sniffed out a dead duck. It's a survival thing for tourists who really have no business taking vacation in this type of climate. We did note that there were a number of small lizards zig-zagging over the walls and daring each other to crawl as close to the humans as possible. Lizards are fine, mostly. Seeing them in the wild is actually quite pleasant and feels like an authentic part of wildlife. Seeing them two inches above the place that your face will be sleeping is the equivalent to challenging T-Rex to a staring contest. Mike took note of my widened black-hole eyes and transformed himself into the savage Viking that he became when I needed protecting. As though he had done it a thousand times before, he grabbed a wicker garbage bin and placed it snug against the wall underneath the creeping lizard. He clenched his fist and with a swift pound on the wall, the lizard fell into the bin like an apple dropping from a tree. I had a knight in shining armour and my mom to look over me. For a country under martial law, I had never felt more secure.

Mom told us to come back up to her house once we got settled. We assumed she was going to read us a bedtime story and warm up sweet milk on the stove for us. We were right about both. She had pulled out a number of books from her collection on the British Royal Family. She happily flipped through photos of Queen Elizabeth and a number of other monarch members who we didn't recognize. Our grandmothers were into the Royals, and I hear the girl from *Suits* has shaken things up with her daring outspokenness and desire to wear nail polish. Otherwise, my extent of familiarity with the faces on the pages was obsolete. The books from 1987 told stories of people who wore hats more elaborate than our Christmas tree and had more rules to follow than a bad kid in an orphanage. It was Mom's way of connecting on what she thought was common ground. Though we had exactly zero interest or knowledge of the Royals, Mom wanted us to feel at ease and this was her way of expressing her recognition of us. Or maybe she was just Mom being Mom.

Over the next couple of days, Mom would show us places to visit on the map and areas to stay away from. She offered history on the great wall that was built around the city and hugged us before bedtime. We took family photos together and looked into one another's eyes. I was so touched by our Thai Mom's care-taking and concern, I wondered if she had children of her own who were travelling the globe and hoped that someone was out there offering the same hospitality.

When it came time to leave, she drove us around Chiang Mai before dropping us off to make sure we understood the layout of the city, never going above 40 kilometres an hour and hands consistently gripped at 10 and two. It was hard to say goodbye to Mom. I knew it would be unlikely we saw one and other again and her thoughtfulness was that memorable kind that you think about years later. Maybe she thought we were the King and Queen of Canada, or maybe she thought we looked like we could use a dose of maternal love. Either way, our hearts and memories remain with Mom and we hope one day to revisit our lizard hut and drive slowly together again.

DUCK FEET AT MIDNIGHT

I was feeling pretty good about catching a lizard. It was such a smooth and calculated manoeuvre that worked perfectly. If James Bond had to capture a lizard in any of his movies, I'd expect the director to ask me about my faultless method. I held my head a little higher than normal and puffed out my chest. I didn't know it in the moment, but that trick would fail 100 per cent of the time in my future attempts. And there were A LOT of attempts. Sleeping in a room *without* copious amounts of lizards in Thailand would be a rarity. It gets to the point where you just go with the flow and smile as you count and name the reptiles in your bedroom while you turn out the light to sleep. That or live in fear. We did a little of both. It's fine and cute when "Bernie" is on the wall 15 feet across the room. But when Big-B starts to make his way towards you with his sticky little hands, things get dicey.

Either way, I had just Jason Bourne(d) a lizard and was off to find food for my wife. I thought maybe I'd find a cheeseburger. We had been pounding the Thai food back for the last few weeks so our insides were a constant stream of erupting volcanoes. I wanted something that would do the opposite. Maybe a brick of cheese. A big, delicious bacon and cheddar covered burger sounded like it would do the trick and block us up a little.

I left the hotel and walked along the side of the road in search of our great meal. We were on the outskirts of the city, the kind of spot you stay before or after a flight. The restaurants I could see all appeared to be closed. I kept walking. The further I went, the more my surroundings seemed to change. Every step brought a little more spray paint, a little more broken glass and boarded up windows. It doesn't happen often, but every once in a while instinct will kick in and give a definitive "Get the fuck outta here" kind of vibe.

> **TRAVEL TIP:** *An important part of being a good traveller is listening to your intuition. I've felt it in San Jose, Costa Rica, as the sun started to set and we could sense the ghouls starting to awaken. We'd felt it in Bangkok when something on the other side of a bridge felt a little stabby.*

I started to feel it there too. It was more a baseball bat to the knee type of feeling but it didn't matter. I was riding too high on my Godzilla-capturing moment to recognize or give in to the sensation.

I kept walking till I found a woman set up on the side of the street selling food. Sometimes those little street vendors have the best food you'll ever come across. In Phi Phi we had pad thai from an old woman that cost $2 and was better than any meal I'd ever tasted. On Khaosan Road in Bangkok, we had massaman curry for about the same price. Every bite felt like a dream. I figured that this lady would be the same. I'd find some magical meal that I'd bring home to Kristen and she'd think I was capable of shooting lightning from my hands like Thor.

There was no one around in any direction. The streets were barren, not even a car drove by. I stepped up to the lady, smiled and said *"Sawasdee ka!"*—the general greeting for "hello" in Thai. She nodded and smiled. The menu was written in Thai and there were no pictures of the food. "Ummm . . . Do you have pad thai?" I asked.

She shook her head. "English?" I asked.

She shook her head again.

Typically, in every spot we'd been till then, every person we'd gotten a meal from or had any "touristy" transaction with, could speak at least a little English. I realized that this was not where the tourists came. This was where Thais broke bottles, spray-painted old buildings and smashed windows. This was not likely the best place for a tall, hairy Canadian who stood out like a monkey in an alligator cage.

I decided the best bet was to grab whatever looked half decent and get the hell out of there. That's when I heard it—a rumbling and buzzing sound growing louder by the second. The baseball bat to the knee feeling grew exponentially. I looked behind me to see a swarm of motorbikes approaching, 20 or 30 of them. I quickly turned to look at the food options in front of me. The bikes pulled in and parked around me and the lady. It was a Thai biker gang.

They wore matching leather jackets and looked about as scary as you'd expect a Thai biker gang in the middle of a shady area late at night to look.

I looked back at the lady and pointed at what appeared to be a bag of soup hanging on a pole with various other pre-prepared meals. She handed me the bag and I handed her way more money than what it was worth. The lady said something aloud in Thai, not the usual "Thank you," but something I'd never heard in a transaction before. It was almost as if she was saying it to the others. I turned around and realized they were surrounding me. Every single one of them. I let out a "How's she going, boys?" hoping that a standard East Coast colloquial greeting would ease the tension. Each of them stared me down with a psychopathic death glare. Up until this point in time, being friendly had gotten me through every pickle I'd ever found myself in. There was no reason to stop now. I whipped out an exaggerated smile and turned my head side to side nodding to the ones closest to me. To them I was either two sandwiches short of a picnic, or an absolute lunatic who feared nothing. I put my head down and started to walk through them. My body tingled and I waited for it. My senses had warned me not to come here but I failed to listen. Now my knees would pay the price.

I don't know if it was because I paid $20 for something that was probably 30 cents and the Thai lady granted me permission not to get the shit beat out of me, but I walked through the gang without incident. They stared me down but no one did a thing.

Once I was past them I started to run. I held on to the bag of whatever the hell I had for dear life. Whatever it was, it was Thai food, so it was hard to go wrong.

When I got back to our room, I was soaked and visibly shaken.

"Are you okay?!" Kristen asked.

"Oh yeah, I'm fine . . . just had a little run in with a Thai biker gang," I said.

I told her the story. "And you still got me food!"

I smiled. "Of course!" I said. "I don't know what it is, but I'm sure it's delicious."

I passed her the bag. In the light of the room I could see inside. I could see what I had purchased.

Duck feet.

I had brought home my wife a bag of chopped off duck feet.

Let's just say that again.

Duck. Feet.

In a broth.

Uncooked. Not that that makes a difference.

Eight of them.

Eight feet chopped off various ducks.

And big. Large duck feet. For my wife.

I went to a gas station—in the opposite direction—and got chips and some Taylor Swift ice cream bars. We couldn't do it. We couldn't bring ourselves to eat them. And I think that's fair. When forced by a Thai gang to make an impulse purchase and that purchase ends up being the feet of duck in a bag of broth, I think it's okay not to eat them. I think that's an okay rule to live by.

KRISTEN GOES TO CAPE BRETON:
Love Story #5

When I was in Grade 11, my basketball team competed in a tournament hosted by Margaree Forks High School in Cape Breton. We stayed at a quaint B&B that had a replica of Farley Mowat's *The Boat Who Wouldn't Float* on the front yard and was run by apple-doll owners who fuelled us with pancakes and fresh biscuits. It was my first impression of Cape Breton and memorable enough that I was looking forward to going back.

Mike grew up in a small town like I did, except his parents lived "downtown." I lived with the out-skirting farmers and probable witness protection people. Inverness county employs a number of fisher-folk who work their claws off during the summer and put their feet up in the winter. I had friends that fished lobster in Mike's hometown and had visited them from time to time. Once, while staying with them, I discovered I had an allergy to lobster. If you're from Nova Scotia, this is as bad as being allergic to air. After throwing up enough shellfish to fill the SkyDome, I accepted the fate that labeled me as a poor example of an East Coaster. This was the same trip that I saw Mike's band play at The Hoff. I arrived at the show looking like a dead body, having spent the entire day before vomiting up seafood. I was glad I dragged myself out though. Although unknowingly, it *was* the night I saw my future husband for the first time. I also learned that Mike's dad worked at the bar as a bouncer. He must have spent 90 per cent of his shift breaking up fights if my first experience was the norm.

I don't know if I met Dougie Ryan the evening I was at the Hoff, but from what I had heard from Mike's friends, if I had met him, I would have surely remembered. Dougie seemed like a legendary, almost mythical townsman according to the folklore floating around. Most of the stories were about him yelling profanity in any given circumstance or exhibiting general characteristics of anger. It all seems very exaggerated to me, as Mike had the demeanour of an angelic kitten. But Dougie stories were consistent and frequent, always told with great excitement and need to reassure the listener that, "they swear to God it's true." I felt like it was time to see for myself.

I invited myself to meet Mike's parents. Curiosity had gotten the best of me. Plus, I was in the depths of lust and felt like a four-hour drive to a tiny beach town was well worth the slim risk of things going sideways. Usually, you meet the parents for brunch or a casual walk in the park. I opted to stay for an entire weekend in their home.

At that time, Inverness was a lazy coastal community with sparkly trinket shops, thick accents, and plenty of unemployed locals who were forced to come and go to find work. Many islanders worked "out West" where oil and jobs were abundant. The town's main road is lined with essential businesses and "Town Heroes." Town Heroes are local residents that offer that authentic touch to the place their bloodline has called home for five generations. In Inverness, most of these people have recognized nicknames and the stories of how they came to be. This population of locals were the inspiration behind Mike's band name—The Town Heroes—a tribute to the few who would never know the recognition they've been awarded. In my hometown there was "Leatherback" and "Kevvy" and I realized every small town must have their notable heroes. I understood this place and felt at home immediately.

I pulled up to Mike's house at 34 Hillcrest and giggled at the cat party on his front steps. If there was anything I had heard repeatedly about Mike's parents it was Dougie: Angry; Caroline: Cats.

I meandered to the front door and was greeted by Caroline, Mike's mother who was beaming with curiosity. I didn't know much about Mike's dating history but it seemed as though there weren't many girlfriends brought home. Mike was leaning against the kitchen cupboards in the distance, awkwardly looking as though he was waiting his turn to greet me.

Before we had time to say hello, Caroline had ushered me into the living room and was fretting over my thirst, level of comfort, how my drive was, if I noticed the new flower boxes that were arranged by the town's garden committee, and did I want to meet Tiger, another cat. The childhood home had furniture decorated in floral panels and endless photos of the three boys—Michael, Timmy and David—covering the wallpaper and panelling. The stomping I could hear in the distance grew louder and soon a towering man with knees that sounded like my bicycle wheel on the season's first ride, emerged and towered over me. "Hi Kristen!" Dougie grumble-yelled while looking at the floor.

I am usually a fairly "huggy" person, especially when meeting new people and *especially* when those new people are my new boyfriend's parents, but I knew my limits and this was one of them. Ten years later, Dougie will now offer a one-armed, millisecond half hug, while staring at the floor, so I think I've made progress.

More and more cats emerged, all of whom had suitable names and histories. The grey cat was named Smokey, the smallest, sweetest cat was named Sweetie, the one who looked like an Ewok was called Ewok, and then there was Tiger. Tiger was a 35-pound tabby who loved humans and hated cats. He was a rescue, like all seven of Caroline's cats, and had gone through a phase of nonstop eating when he first landed at the feline boarding home. He ate and ate until he quadrupled in size. Tiger was immediately my favourite. I felt like we understood each other.

I was excited to see the town and to finally say hello to Mike. With a hug only slightly more forthcoming than his father's, we embraced in the kitchen and I was offered my 15th cup of tea since I landed half an hour earlier. I felt like I was at a B&B all over again. Maybe it was a Cape Breton thing? I wondered if there would be pancakes and biscuits.

Our first order of business was driving "the strip." I had done this during my food poisoning/getting struck by lightning trip, so was familiar with this being a mandatory activity. You hadn't done Inverness if you hadn't done the strip. It's like driving the Vegas strip except the sights in Inverness include Ivan's convenience store, the Bear Paw gift shop, the Dollar Store and a Credit Union that had just received $50,000 for a renovation that apparently it didn't need and the locals were pissed about. We saw several Town Heroes—Speed Bump, Arthur Hawk, and Chi Chi—before leaving the town limits to travel further up the Cabot Trail.

Our first stop was in the neighbouring community of Cheticamp. This primarily French–Acadian community is supported by the fishing industry and spattered with businesses that make a tourist town run. I was hoping to grab a coffee for the drive, and though I'm not a huge Tim Hortons fan, I spotted one in the distance and asked if we could pull over.

"We can," Mike said, "but everyone's gonna stare at us."

I was familiar with small-town curiosity. I would be "the new girl" and people would make note of that—nothing out of the ordinary and certainly nothing bothersome. Tim Hortons are the mecca of cheap doughnuts, mediocre coffee, and always full to the gills with people over 60 who spend most of their time, money, and social interaction within its four walls. It survives on people who smoke a pack a day and drink cups of sugar drizzled in coffee to wash them down. I had been to many Tim's over the years and this they all had in common.

Pulling open the heavy door, we could see that every single person in Cheticamp was inside. It must have been a retirement party or Bingo day. It was a hum of French colloquialisms, burly laughter, and lots and lots of rubber boots. The door made a small thud as it shut behind us and in less than a moment, the time it takes for a lion to eat a hotdog, the doughnut shop fell to a funeral-like silence. An entire town's worth of eyes were looking at us. Silent thoughts were swirling around, judging us, and reaching conclusions. I didn't know if I felt like a movie star or Hannibal Lecter. I looked up at Mike who gave me the "I told you so" nod as he ordered my coffee. With some version of the order I had hoped for, we backed out in moderate haste. "What the hell just happened?!" I shouted. "Cheticamp," Mike replied.

The Cabot Trail is a 298-kilometre stretch of road that twists and turns through the rugged landscape of the Cape Breton highlands. I had been here once before, but I was only a fetus. When my mom was eight months pregnant, she toured the Cabot Trail on the back of a motorcycle. I used to think my sense of adventure came from my dad but realized now that she was just as much a daredevil as he was. We were heading towards the famous Skyline Trail—a picturesque hiking trail, complete with mountain views, ocean air, and moose bigger than Farley Mowat's un-floating boat. I didn't know the hiking trail would be so technical. Comparatively speaking, it's quite simple, but I was expecting a leisurely stroll on a beaten path. Maybe a butterfly would land on the tip of my finger as I outstretched it, or a gentle breeze would pick up and blow blossoms into my hair, so I looked like a filtered photo. I had borrowed a dress from a friend for my weekend getaway and because this was the planned outfit, it was the one I was wearing on that day. There was no back-up hiking clothing, so in my miniskirt dress I went.

The hike was like entering a children's book or National Geographic photo essay. We saw wildlife, wildflowers, and I'm pretty sure at least a mosquito landed on my fingertip. I took pictures and did my best to seem funny and cool. I thought about how my hometown had only cows and senior citizens to offer, fields of wheat and fields of old, rusted-out Chevys from the 70s that someone said they'd fix up one day and never did. Cape Breton was a magical place. There was deep, midnight blue ocean as far as I could see and it smelled like new beginnings and cotton candy in the air. I was so thrilled that my fella was from such a place. If all went well, I would get to come back here.

On our way back into Inverness, I had to get another glimpse of Cheticamp. Maybe word had spread that the movie stars were coming back. I didn't want to disappoint the townspeople and was also getting hungry. Mike asked if I liked fried chicken as there was a mom and pop shop that came recommended. He would learn that day that fried chicken was my favourite. Fried chicken was my birthday meal, my preferred period snack, my emotional eating go-to, my celebratory dish and my reliable comfort food. Yes, in fact, I loved fried chicken.

The chicken shop had a local bulletin board hung in the entryway. While you wait for your meal, you could shop for a dog walker or buy an old lawnmower. Maybe a Dodge Neon that just needed some fixing up and was listed for $500 obo. But the poster that caught my eye was one that was selling worms. It read "Worms: 10 for $1 or 20 for $2." Whoever had crafted this marketing masterpiece was clearly on their way to the top. A decade later I am still enamoured with it.

People admire the simplicity of the Cape Breton lifestyle and find ease in the ocean. Cape Bretoners invite their neighbours over for tea and sponsor the school soccer team. It's a place that Mike is proud to be from and that welcomed me with open arms and enormous cats. It's the place we would fall in love.

FIRST TIME IN COSTA RICA:
Make Hay While the Sun Shines

One of the reasons we travel is because we know we won't be able to do it forever. At some point we'll be too old, too sick, too this, too that. Anything can happen along the way; we might as well do the things we enjoy while we can.

In Costa Rica, we rented a weird little half-car-half-jeep whose brand name neither of us had heard of before. We knew in advance we wouldn't be splurging on GPS so I pretended it was 1998 and printed off Google Maps pages of the entire country. While every person we talked to beforehand said it was 100 per cent NECESSARY AND EXTREMELY IMPORTANT, we figured we'd go without it since we're cheap bastards and would rather save a few extra bucks for fresh coconuts.

Driving without GPS in Costa Rica is kind of like driving around the moon looking for a grey rock. Road signs had been installed just two years prior. They were generally as efficient as The Undertaker in a game of hide 'n seek. When driving along a straight road with pre-existing knowledge of exactly where to go, ample signs would confirm you were on the correct route. The general signage tone in these scenarios was a "You got this bud, keep 'er rollin'!" type message. But, when you came to a spot with more than one option to turn, the Costa Rican Sign Department decided to put it up to chance. At 100 per cent of intersections, there were zero signs. "Oh, you've come to a spot on the road with six turning options, no people, structures, or general landmarks in sight? Good luck!"

It almost felt like a deliberate little fuck you to tourists. But the joke was on them. I had the pages. Well . . . sort of. We didn't really know where we'd be going in Costa Rica other than our first and last stops. Everything in between was open for wherever adventure took us. This meant I had hundreds of pages of various routes, destinations, landmarks, highways, roads and potential places we *may* end up. This made my map job a bit more difficult. I had to use librarian-like execution to sort through the 40 pounds of paper to find something resembling the route we decided upon. The bulk of the trip was just me giving Kristen reassuring thumbs up gestures as she drove and I tried to make sense of the shitstorm at my feet before we ended up down a wrong road and forced to smuggle drugs for a Panamanian cartel.

> **TRAVEL TIP:** *Plan anything you can in advance. Sometimes you want to leave things up to chance, but with the things you know you'll be doing, get an idea of what/ where/when/how before you leave so you don't waste time and energy while you're on the road. Also, find a place you can print things for free. Whether you have a spot yourself, or your cousin's girlfriend works for the government and will give you free pages if you let her borrow your massage gun, if you don't have to, don't pay for printing.*

At forks in the road, we tried to just trust our gut. This also forced us to stop and talk to locals. And I'm glad we did. It led us to places and friendly folk we wouldn't have come across otherwise. Kristen can speak Spanish well enough to converse. If you're looking for someone to order "two chicken platters with beans" I'm the guy. Anything other than that, I just nod or shake my head depending on whether I perceive the situation to be going good (nod) or bad (shake).

The first people we asked for directions from was a group of Jehovah's Witnesses in Liberia. They were standing there handing out bibles and pamphlets doing what they do everywhere in the world: trying to convince completely uninterested people going about their day to change their religion on the spot. Between that and their equally ineffective door-knocking, I never understood how at the end of the year when they get together at their big AGM, they decide to maintain their current course.

I picture the meeting to go basically like this:

Head of the Jehovah Witnesses: "So . . . looks like we knocked on 12,346,788 doors this year and interacted with over ten million on the streets. The conversion rate was . . . let me see . . . . Looks like zero per cent for the 66th year in a row. Interesting. Anyone have any ideas of what we should do as a group moving forward?"

Everyone at conference: "KEEP KNOCKING ON DOORS AND HANDING OUT PAMPHLETS ON THE STREET!" followed by an eruption of cheers and fist pumping.

The Jehovahs on the street in Liberia were kind and generous and pointed us exactly in the right direction. No matter where in the world you come across them, they'll help you out if they can. Great people.

The first place we stayed at was an eco-resort in Bijagua. I later learned that no one else in Costa Rica seemed to know where this place was. I was even pronouncing it right with the "J" like a throaty H. People would look at us like we made it up—kind of like Clarence in Nova Scotia.

Bijagua was beautiful and we hiked through a jungle that felt like Jurassic Park. We stayed in a little cabin in the woods with animals all around us. There was a tree older than God himself and when it rained, I just leaned back and let it wash over me.

We stumbled upon a troop of a few dozen monkeys on the property where we were staying. As we watched on, we saw a single monkey swing towards them through the trees in the distance. He approached the group and a massive fight between him and another male began. It was a full-on brawl and loud as a train wreck. They squealed, clawed, and threw looping haymakers like two drunken middle-aged men settling an old score from a high school hockey rivalry 20 years earlier. In the end, it appeared as though the new guy won. The loser swung to another tree and looked back, his whole world behind him. His family, his lovers, his friends. The other monkeys began to taunt him. They squealed and hollered and he sat there defeated. I don't speak much monkey, but knew enough to understand that he wasn't coming back.

A new alpha male had arrived. He fought off the previous king and took his throne. The loser would wander through the woods on his own.

He'd try to find a new group to join but was likely too old to be able to fight off a young leader. He'd likely live the rest of his days on his own, in the jungle, thinking of the past when he ruled, when he was king of it all. That morning when he woke up he had no idea what would happen. He was on top and in his eyes would be forever. That changed in a second.

We left the mysterious Bijagua and hit the standard tourist spots like the Arenal volcano and La Fortuna waterfall. We went to a coastal town called Samara and met up with a lady from North Carolina who had booked me to play a festival in Raleigh two months earlier. Her name was Terri and she was filled with southern energy and charm. She was on an episode of *Matlock* when she was younger and I thought that was pretty cool. Her daughter Aubrey—who was a moderately famous actress herself—was getting married in a week. Terri and Aubrey were down early to spend time together. We met up with them for drinks and listened to a guy with loop pedals think he was Jimi Hendrix but sounded like a dying otter. Kristen went to a "Booty Cardio" class with the gals and I sat by the water drinking cheap beer and watching little crabs come to life on the beach as the sun set.

Terri had said that the country felt like the perfect place to disappear to. I started to feel the pull. I wanted to just get a little hut on the beach, learn to fish, and how to find mangos in the jungle. I'd tame a puma and train it to hunt for us. Kristen could teach yoga and I'd play at all the little restaurants every night for a few bucks and a free meal for both of us. It would be a simple life but we'd be happy.

We had fallen in love with the country—the people, the scenery, the micro-climates. We wanted to figure out how to spend more time there, how to make it a part of our life. I thought of the monkey. I thought of how things can change in an instant and how we wait around so often for things to come to fruition. We wanted to figure out how to do it right away, before we couldn't anymore.

CROSSING THE STREET IN BANGKOK

When in doubt, do what the locals do. This goes for everything from table manners to cultural greetings. It's important to research ahead of time what particular customs, rules, or laws exist in places you're visiting for the first time. Superstitions are rife in some cultures and frowned upon in others. You can save yourself both embarrassment and hassle by familiarizing yourself with local customs. That said, I hadn't thought to put any pre-planning into how one might simply cross the street in Bangkok.

It was less cultural and more cutthroat. Some might argue that it's one and the same when it comes to Bangkok traffic. With a population of almost 10 million, the labyrinth of vehicles widespread with neglected safety inspections, the speeding tuk-tuks escorting multi-generations of families, and Thai men selling bags of crisped crickets, we faced the dismaying challenge of getting from one side of the road to the other.

There were traffic lights, but they acted as more of a suggestion than a rule. We were frozen statues every time the walk light illuminated. Not a single vehicle stopped what it was doing. That was: driving 1,000 miles an hour, tailgating the car in front of it while swerving around bicycles and toddler-sized lizards.

We looked around and observed a few of the locals crossing the street with utter ease. Mostly older men. They were so unfazed, it was as though they were in a walking meditation. They were Yoda, blindfolded and aligning their chakras, while we stood trembling in same spot on the sidelines for 20 minutes.

We decided that if we stood awkwardly close to an old Thai man, basically hugging him, we could "do what he does" and arrive on the other side safely. He would set us a pick, so to speak. We walked so closely and in such unison with these chosen pedestrians, the Rockettes themselves would have envied our precision. This is exactly how we got around Bangkok after that. Each time we approached a streetlight, we'd identify a "safe man" and both Mike and I would basically get a piggyback ride through the insanity, smiling and giving thumbs up when he'd inevitably turn to look at us. We were the shadows of Thai men at every block. It worked effortlessly, every single time. It was like a protection cloak was thrown over our shoulders, a shield that acted as a force field to oncoming traffic. The Thai Street Walkers are the lesser-known heroes of their country, aiding countless incompetent foreigners in their quest towards curry and full-moon parties. We proudly marched beside them, embodying their methodical movements like a flock of synchronized birds.

BABE:

Family, Photos, and Fading Away

Kristen's grandmother Babe lived in a nursing home in rural Nova Scotia. Like all nursing homes, it smelled like Vaseline, dentures, and perm solution. On most days, someone would set off the smoke detector or accidentally press their emergency alert button. But Babe felt at home with her peers there and that's all a person can really ask for.

At the end of her life she developed dementia and genuinely believed a "creature" had become her roommate. "I've never actually seen it but it's a small, grey, fluffy animal with BIG eyes," she'd say, describing in detail the creature she never saw. That's how we found out her mind was going. After searching Babe's place from top to bottom with a flashlight in one hand a hammer in the other (who knew what kind of violence that weird little thing was capable of) we realized what was going on. It's sad as hell to see someone start to fade away, but also pretty damn funny to hear the things they say.

She became fascinated with thinking we'd be on TV. "We have to head out; I have an art show tonight, Nan!" Kristen would say. "Is it going to be on TV?" she'd ask with hopeful enthusiasm. The chances of an art opening at a local dive bar being on primetime American networks was, although optimistic and maybe the proper mindset needed to make it to the top, a far-fetched scenario. One time I actually *was* on TV for a gig. It was the Boston tree-lighting ceremony and broadcast on ABC. Babe saw it and it was game over. From then on, we were basically Anderson Cooper rolled into a Jennifer Aniston and Jerry Seinfeld sandwich. On any channel, at any time, there was potential to see us. "We're heading to our friends for supper tonight," Kristen would tell her. "Well . . . is it going to be on TV?" she'd ask. We felt important thinking that people of the world found us so interesting that our most mundane of tasks were worthy of prime time slots. She kept a watchful eye on CNN and *Little People, Big World*, confident she would see our faces.

Babe was sweet and would do anything for us. Her generosity was sadly taken advantage of many times. She once paid for her neighbour's kid's braces because they showed up at her front door and asked her to. Her kindness was both her greatest quality and biggest weakness. She was also incredibly meticulous about her appearance. Her nickname— Babe—was given to her by her kid sister when Babe was a baby—"Baby Babe." But Babe liked to think it's because she was, in fact, a *babe*. One of her favourite stories to tell was about her first day of school in a new town. "When I stepped off the school bus, all the boys turned their heads and said, 'Woooow'" she'd reminisce, as she unnecessarily reapplied her cherry lipstick. As the wife of politician, Babe spent many years schmoozing at community events, fundraisers and funerals. Everyone knew her and wanted her around. Even in her last years spent at Crosskill Court Nursing Home she was the most popular resident, everyone wanting her to be their card or puzzle partner. She would likely say she was the prettiest resident too.

In Babe's nursing home, I might as well have been Andre the Giant himself. Old women would stare in visible awe at my gargantuan stature, pointing, gasping. "Look at the size of him!" they'd say aloud from their wheelchairs, hunched over and mesmerized. The entire place would come to a standstill. I'd just smile and wave like a celebrity (maybe they saw me on TV?), making the day for those fortunate enough to make eye contact with me. And Babe felt the most special. We'd walk her to lunch and she'd smile wide, all the other old ladies wishing they had their own personal giant to bring them to their shepherd's pie.

Babe was always curious about our adventures and loved to look at pictures. After we got married, we knew showing her a few shots from Jamaica would be the highlight of her day.

The first picture we showed her was the best one we had. We were dressed up, smiling, it was moderately straight, and almost in focus.

"Is that a boat out there?" she asked right away.

The drug dealer/lifeguard we met at the edge of the water who took our pictures—let's just call him David Hasselhoff Escobar, or DHE for short—got a pretty good shot of us in a cute little pavilion. I looked at the picture, straining my eyes to see. In the background, almost microscopic, there was a small dot on the water behind us. It was the tiniest, most insignificant detail of the picture. In most cases, the first thing one might say upon seeing a picture of this nature would be a comment on Kristen's dress, or maybe "Mike, this is the first time I've ever seen you without a T-shirt and looking like a pathetic homeless dirtbag." Some may point out the cement beam of the pavilion or ask a question about the resort. When we showed the picture to Babe she immediately let out an "Oh my God!" We assumed she was amazed by how good we looked on our wedding day. DHE had captured a beautiful moment in time and now others could celebrate it with us.

Her question came with pure amazement and curiosity. We looked towards the tiny dot. "I . . . I . . . guess it is . . ." I said. Out in the water, the place where boats usually go, there was in fact REALLY a boat out there. She never mentioned anything about us or the picture; she was just too fascinated by the unlikely scenario of there being a boat on the water in Jamaica.

She shook her head the way someone would upon hearing about a blind 90-year-old man climbing Everest barefoot and without oxygen, "Isn't that something!"

At the end of her life, we became caretakers for Babe. After she was repeatedly found wandering outside in the middle of the night, she had to leave the nursing home. She moved in with Kristen's dad in their old farm house. We drove two hours each way every week to visit, get groceries, pay bills, and hear her stories. I'd play guitar for her and spend hours on YouTube trying to find the song that, "the cute little boy sings." Googling variations of "cute little boy" made me feel a little weird, but those were all the details we had. And that's what you do for family. You look up weird things on the internet and sing the first verse of "Sonny's Dream" repeatedly if that's what they need.

Before then, I understood family as the people who shared my blood. After marrying Kristen, I realized that it went further. Her blood was mine. The people in her life were now a part of mine, too.

One night on our weekly visit, we woke to the sound of voices downstairs. The wind blew outside, and we thought someone may have left the TV on. We soon realized it was Babe. She was singing. She sat on the edge of her bed and sang the line, "I went down to the water," again and again. She sang in a low, baritone drone much different than her regular voice. It was haunting and beautiful and felt like it was a seminal moment in everything. We listened at the top of the stairs, the melody echoing through the creaky old farm house at 4 a.m.

A week later, Babe passed away. At her service, a stream of people she influenced over her previous 87 years passed through, all of them singing the praises of a kind woman. A 106-year-old man, Dr. Allen, gave the most amazing, eloquent and thoughtful speech I'd ever heard. He wove in anecdotes about Babe, themes about life and dying, and the essence of what it is to be human and how Babe exemplified that. We all laughed, we all cried. He was my new hero.

The night Babe sang felt like it was something special. I took her words and the melody she sang and turned it into a song. A song about death. A song about leaving this world behind and crossing over. A song about going to find her daughter Nancy who passed away five years earlier. I felt like it was something I had to do. A tribute of sorts, an homage to who she was and what she meant to us. I called the song "Babe" and tried my best to capture the feeling of what we heard that night. Kristen did a painting to go along with the song and showcased who Babe was to her. I thought about life, death, and the things we'd been through together so far. I wondered where it would all take us.

PIGDOG:

Love Story #6

At some point in our relationship, I asked the inevitable question, "When did you know you loved me?" We were well into the "I love yous" so I could probe these areas without hesitation.

"I think it was that trip to Cape Breton," Mike smirked, and I knew exactly what he meant.

The Broad Cove Road is 7.5 kilometres of weathered dirt, lined by quiet homes and ocean views. We drove below 50 and listened to our new favourite band, Dry the River, on repeat, our love as thick as the salt in the air.

Suddenly, a PIGDOG appeared out of the woods!

We stopped the car as it crossed in front of us. "Is that a . . . pig . . . dog?" I asked, wondering what the hell kind of clone freak animal I was seeing. The animal had the head of a dog, but the body of a pig—coiled tail, hooves and all. It was medium build, maybe the size of a beagle with short brown fur. It ran across the road with haste, leaving the eye just enough time to spot his pig tail, curled at his behind.

Unless the 14-year-old girl scooping ice cream for a summer job had slipped acid into our respective Moonmist and Heavenly Hash-filled cones, neither of us had consumed psychedelics. We had no idea what it was, but knew that we had seen it.

It crossed in front of us without ever looking in our direction, both of us mesmerized and perplexed at the same time. It scurried into the woods and out of sight forever.

There were so many questions. Where did it come from? Was it a pet? Was there a secret bio-engineering lab in the backwoods of Cape Breton? All of them can essentially be summed up with a definitive "What the hell?" At the end of the day, we know what we saw. It was a pig and it was a dog, a species of animal we, and probably no one, had ever seen before. It was without question, a PIGDOG.

We still talk about it to this day. We rarely bring it up in conversation with others as we agree it sounds ridiculous and there appears to be no knowledge of a local experimentation site. All we know is that somewhere in the backwoods of Cape Breton, a small, weird, half-dog-half-pig roams free.

While this was an unusual animal sighting, it was but one of the remarkable things that happened on that trip. Over the previous days we had encountered several rare animals in Cape Breton: a whale pod in Magic Cove, a snowy owl on Inverness beach, a little red fox and her stolen campground hot dog trotting proudly with dinner hanging from her mouth. The PIGDOG was the show-stopper but the surrealness seemed to permeate throughout the entire island's wildlife.

On the evening of the snowy owl sighting, we roasted salmon on rocks, warmed by our campfire. We smooched under the moonlight, fireworks exploded in the distance, set by townspeople on an ordinary Wednesday night. Another group of people released Chinese lanterns, filled with their hand-written wishes they'd hope became true before summer's end. We knew we were falling in love and it was as though the rest of the world knew it too.

THE TRAGIC DEATH OF BOB MARLEY

Out of the two reggae songs in the world—the one about really, really enjoying marijuana usage, and the other about being a good person, not judging others and being exceptionally happy—I'm equally impartial to both. I can't say I'm a giant fan but I don't completely despise it. To me, there's something strange about a genre of music that's *always* happy. I just want to hear one reggae song about a bad day. Maybe about a trip to the dentist or the time you ordered sneakers on Amazon and they were the wrong size. Something we can all relate to.

When we were in Jamaica we decided to do a tour of Bob Marley's house. It would be fun to learn about Jamaica's most famous export, and while reggae may not totally be my forté, Marley had certainly crossed into a realm of pop-culture fame few on our planet ever achieve. Stepping into his former stomping grounds might just let us mingle with whatever magic he had touched.

Our shuttle drive there was generally uneventful other than watching a man with a machete go on a rampage in a small town. I never saw exactly what happened since we were in motion, but he was starting to swing at people as we passed by. I felt pretty good at least getting to see that much.

When we got to the infamous Marley estate, we had a bit of time to kill. The night before, we met another Canadian couple who talked and talked and wouldn't let anyone else get a word in. They were so annoying we kept poking each other under the table each time they said something dumb. At the end of the conversation, they gave us a handful of weed. If that never happened, our opinion of them being "nice enough people" would have clearly fallen along the lines of "pompous shits."

While we waited for the tour to begin, Kristen tried some weed from the fairly decent Canadians. Within minutes she was on a rocket-ship blistering through the synapses of space and time. The drug was exponentially stronger than anything in Canada. She glazed over and I realized I'd be doing the talking from then on out.

As this happened, our tour guide came to get us. His name was Captain Crazy. He was tall and probably in his 50s. He was also drunk beyond belief and could barely stand up. It was nine in the morning. He had the most unique laugh I'd ever heard. I couldn't quite pinpoint if it was that of a villain or just a stoned Rastafarian, but it sounded like a cartoon hyena's orgasm. It was three elongated "Haaaaaas" each time, with the first being most prominent and subsequently getting weaker: "HAAAAAAAA haaaaaaaa haaaa!" Everything he said was followed by a definitive HAAAAAAAA haaaaaaaa haaaa! He could barely stand he was so drunk and his eyes were glassy with a hint of something akin to meth—as any good guide should be first thing in the morning. I liked him. He *could have* woken up and had a drink or two before work, smoked a joint, and gotten a slight buzz on. He *could have* waited until at least lunch to get into the hard drugs. But Captain Crazy went all out. He drank ALL the booze and smoked ALL the crack. He was a "meth at sunrise" kind of guy and his dedication to go all in was admirable. If there was anyone who could tell us about Bob Marley, he was the guy.

On the drive to the tour, I realized I didn't really know anything about Bob. I knew he was from Jamaica, played reggae music, and was now dead. By the end of the tour, my knowledge of Bob Marley would be the exact same. I knew there was a particular rock that he liked to sit on periodically, and that he was at one point a palm reader, but that's about it. Captain Crazy was easily the worst tour guide to ever live. Bob Marley's corpse would have been a more informative guide.

The tour started with a band set up playing Bob Marley songs. The criteria to be in the band were as follows: Be over 80, have no more than five teeth, have the ability to play incredibly happy music while looking sad, and to be able to play an instrument without moving any muscles other than the ones necessary to create sounds.

It was the saddest thing I'd ever seen. I felt weird inside knowing every little thing clearly was *not* alright. I'm not sure if it was some form of imprisonment or torture for them, but there were some obvious indicators that they did not want to be there. "The best band in Jamaica, mon!" Captain Crazy said. Somewhere, I assumed snipers had guns pointed at their heads if they tried to flee.

On a typical tour, a guide will give bits of information, take you from one location to the next, answer any questions and look after the general well-being of all involved on the tour. Captain Crazy had a slightly different technique. His method was to sporadically do his strange laugh, drink rum from a paper bag, and dance in circles while our tour group wandered around the property. Both are acceptable methods, it depends on each individual person to choose which works for them.

When a question was posed to Captain Crazy, he did, to the best of his ability, try to answer.

"When was marijuana deemed legal here?" one curious tour patron asked. Captain Crazy sat down and told us all to sit in a circle with him. I figured this was the point where it all changed. I was ready to be enlightened. He hushed us all, gave his patented laugh and said, "Weed is the gift of life, mon!"

"But was there a specific date when it became legal in Jamaica?" the man asked.

"No, mon! The day I was born weed was legal!"

As good an answer as any, I suppose.

As our scattered group walked on their own through the grounds, Kristen and I came across Bob's gravesite. Captain Crazy happened to be there. I put my hand on the grave and felt the energy in the room.

"How did Bob die?" I asked. I don't know what I was expecting. I should have known that Captain Crazy's total incompetence would not change the moment *I* spoke up.

"Bob live forever, mon," he informed me.

"In our heads, yes," I said, "but what happened on earth to cause him to be in this particular situation . . . buried in the earth in front of us."

"Bob is all around us, mon."

That's the closest I got to an answer. I, to this day, have no idea how Bob actually died. If Captain Crazy woke up and didn't chug a bottle of rum and snort some meth, I might have more answers. But what's life with all the answers? This way I can just make up my own stories about Bob and his life. I can imagine him riding a tiger and dying of Lyme disease from a tick bite. I picture him trekking through Antarctica, inventing the internet, climbing Everest with a hoodie and bag of joints. That's the Bob Marley I picture. Maybe that's why Captain Crazy didn't tell us anything, to let our imaginations run wild.

I never found out what happened to Bob Marley, but that's okay. What I do know is he played reggae music, was from Jamaica, and wasn't alive anymore. In the end, I suppose that's more than enough. When I die, if every person in the world knows that I was Canadian, played music, and somehow died, I'd be happy with that legacy.

SEATTLE'S SILVER LININGS

I'm basically a travel agent when it comes to booking accommodations. Aside from the time I cried in San Jose, Costa Rica, when we arrived at our jail-cell of a hotel room, I've been fairly consistent in seeking out great places to stay. I've heard some travellers argue that accommodations aren't that important. "You'll be out exploring anyways, so who cares about your room?" I used to think like that. In my 20s, I spent many a night in shared hostel rooms with strangers, all of whom could have easily robbed me or worse. Or that place in Belize where I had to hop over a giant rat in the middle of the night to get to the bathroom. Or in Nicaragua where the bed bugs outnumbered the thread count on the linens. While our hotel in Seattle wasn't *that* bad, it wasn't Versailles either. Your accommodations are, however, both your first impression and home base of a new place.

> **TRAVEL TIP:** *I've learned that after a long flight or day spent on your feet, there's nothing quite like a comfortable room. If something goes awry (you ate duck feet or shit yourself in public) you'll be grateful for a clean, safe home base.*

My hotel must-haves: walking distance to places we want to see, private bathroom, safe and interesting neighbourhoods, close to the airport if we have an early flight, clean, free breakfast, and bonus points for something interesting about it. One time we stayed in a rock n' roll-themed room that blasted "We Will Rock You" every time we opened the door. That's the kind of selling feature I swoon over. Our hotel in Seattle advertised everything but the singing door, all for under $150 a night.

Sometimes the online pictures are more complimentary than the real deal. Kind of like photos on Tinder or McDonald's commercials. With paint peeling everywhere, the pool closed for repairs, and side streets loud with construction, our hotel room in Seattle was less than impressive. The bedsheets were made from cheap, slippery (not in a fun way) polyester, and the "deck" was a rooftop covered in tarry garbage and old mattresses. For breakfast, you had to walk outside, around the building into a beige-painted room that served plasticky-white bagels and boiled eggs kept in the fridge for an unknown period of time.

But there's always a bright side, even to the most Bates' of hotels. The woman at the front counter lent us her umbrella to protect us from the Seattle elements and we were a five-minute walk from the best fudge in town. There were also re-runs of those "so-bad-they're-good" Hallmark Christmas movies on all night long. The silver lining was found in Candace Cameron's snowflake cookies—the envy of cold eggs and rubbery bread everywhere.

The city itself hosts an energy of both grit and glam. The graffitied walls of night clubs and back allies of the '90s grunge era lingers amidst the botanical biospheres of Amazon's futuristic headquarters. We paid a visit to the Crocodile, a space of nostalgia, plaid shirts and familiar album covers where a local musician who doubled as our bus boy, offered a private tour of the legendary venue. Since 1991, music fans far and wide have recognized the Crocodile as Seattle's best live music venue.

"There is no other spot in the Pacific Northwest with such a storied and beloved past, and no other rock and roll venue that has earned its right to occupy the hearts of so many," boasts the Crocodile's website. Countless incredible bands played there, including: Nirvana, Pearl Jam, Cheap Trick, R.E.M., Mudhoney, and Yoko Ono. Though the rooms are now filled with everything from burlesque to bingo, we had the place to ourselves to experience our own 15 minutes of fame.

Mike stood on the iconic stage where Kurt Cobain and so many of his other influences did before him. Legends were made there. Bands and their music that will live on forever got their start in that room. He leaned down and rubbed the stage for good luck. The room was empty but you could feel the lingering energy from countless nights of euphoria throughout. The ghosts of a thousand bands and parties past swirled around, Mike trying to lean into their secrets. I could feel them too. I knew he was standing in a place with a history that made him who he was. A shitty hotel's a worthy exchange for such an opportunity. We bought a T-shirt and imprinted the moment forever in our minds.

We visited the familiar attractions too. The famous Pike Place Market where fish is thrown and fresh chowder is served in edible bowls. The Pop Culture Museum displays Prince's purple velvet jumpsuits and the International Fountain spit water choreographed to music. The glass sculptures found at Chihuly Garden was like the set of a Dr. Seuss film, gleaming with vibrant colour and reflective curiosity. The touristy areas serve their purpose and combined with colourful obscurities like street ping-pong and thrift store shopping that can be found in Seattle's South Park district (which also claims a crime rate that is 187-per cent higher than the national average), you're bound to have a fulsome experience. This has been our rule of thumb in most places we've visited, a hybrid of attractions and off the beaten track secret spaces seems to promise a satisfying sensory journey. Buying Starbucks in Seattle might be on the bucket list, but chatting with the homeless guy in the chicken costume is more memorable.

Our final night in Seattle was shared with friends who I had met in Costa Rica at a yoga retreat. Cathy and Patricia treated us to a seafood dinner in a classy restaurant that overlooked the harbour. A place we normally couldn't afford, making it all the more adventurous and a good excuse to dig out any remaining clothing from our backpacks that weren't covered in mustard stains or wrinkled as a bulldog. When we slid into the shiny, dirty-pimp sheets at our 1.5 star hotel—misleadingly advertised as a 4-star—a sense of ease washed over my limbs. I cracked open the leftover box of fudge and clicked on *Marry Me at Christmas* to set the stage for my final Seattle dreamscape.

TRYING NEW THINGS:

The Great White Hope

The national sport in Thailand is Muay Thai kick-boxing. Kids begin training as soon as they can walk. Some will have 300 fights by the time they're 20. It's ingrained in their DNA and at the forefront of their culture. I've always had a fascination with martial arts. I love the competitive aspect behind it. When you're in the ring or cage it's just you and your will against that of your opponent. No one can change the outcome other than you. It's the ultimate test of heart and what you're willing to endure. Although I never met him, my grandfather was a boxer in the navy. I've always had some type of curiosity for hand-to-hand combat running through my blood.

In Chiang Mai, I decided that I'd go to a gym to train for a day. At the very least I'd get a workout in and get to say I did it. That was all I really wanted. I found a gym online that was about an hour walk away. It looked perfect. Everything on its website was written in broken English and the head trainer appeared to be smoking in most of the pictures. I kissed Kristen on the forehead and left. She was going to meet a Thai medicine woman with magic hands she met the day before.

That sunny day it was 47 degrees Celsius. Four seconds after I stepped outside, I was a puffy ball of disgusting wet. I looked like a freezer burnt hot-dog bun that you heated up too long in the microwave so it's fucked both ways. My face was beet red and everything spun. In Canada, getting into the 30s is a rarity. Forty-fucking-seven degrees. And humid. Every breath was a sticky struggle to get oxygen to my lungs.

I had mapped out the route in my head and was fairly certain of how to get to there. I knocked off my mental landmarks: a bridge, a river, key street names. By the time I arrived at the gym my eyes were burning from the constant stream of sweat. I was out of breath and panting. My legs were heavy and arms like rubber.

I was ready to be a kick boxer.

I met the smoking trainer when I walked inside. He was probably in his fifties and looked like a villain the Italian Stallion would have fought if they'd ever made a Rocky movie about a trip to Thailand that goes wrong. His face was leathery and scarred and if he ever smiled in his life he certainly didn't do it in front of a tourist at his gym. He was perfect.

I told him I was there to train for the day. I paid him the fee, the equivalent to about $3.

"To start, you go run five mile now!" he said once the business transaction was done.

I didn't know where to begin. Should I just point to myself? Look at this fat, sweaty mess! You want ME to run five miles? Sitting down and breathing in the heat was almost intolerable. The chances of me running five miles and not spontaneously combusting into a ball of flames were exactly zero per cent. I would veritably explode. Every organ would just say fuck it and go out with a literal bang. I would be there and then I wouldn't. The Thais who saw my fateful end would tell of a tall, white, kinda fat and incredibly sweaty man who evaporated into the ether as he strode along at a slower than normal jogging pace.

I also had the option to point out that I didn't even have sneakers. You want ME to run five miles in flip-flops? That's the route I decided to go. Probably the easier one.

I pointed to my feet and shook my head. "No sneakers!"

He walked over to a counter of gear and grabbed a skipping rope. "Thirty minute," he said as he handed it to me.

I took the rope and started. I knew I couldn't do 30 minutes of skipping in 47 degrees. I probably couldn't do 30 minutes in any degrees. A minute in and my calves were burning. The mat around me was drenched and I felt the BIG ONE coming on. I had to get at least 10 minutes. I thought of *Rocky* 1 through 4. Sometimes a good underdog movie is all you need. In *Cinderella Man*, Russel Crowe had to fight an *actual* fight without any food in his belly. The three plates of bacon I had just consumed at our unlimited hotel buffet could get me through a couple jumps with a skipping rope.

Seven minutes. My arms were almost non-functional. I was so thirsty I started to stick out my tongue and catch the salty drops from my forehead.

I got to 10 minutes and stopped. My body was gassed. Every bit of it. The heat was too much. I took a drink from my water bottle and tried to catch my breath. The trainer was off with another fighter, an actual Thai trying to climb the ranks. I stood around drinking water for a few minutes before another trainer came over. "You finish?" he asked. He was short and stocky with thick legs that probably kicked down a few trees in their day.

"Thirty minutes," I told him.

He nodded his head in approval. I wasn't quite sure where things would go from there but I knew I didn't have much left in me. Ten minutes of skipping was maybe good enough. There couldn't be much more to a workout than that.

The trainer pointed to the ring and nodded towards it. He passed me some hand wraps and gloves and we entered the sacred space.

In my life time, my total experience in training any type of combat sport is one month at a boxing gym. We covered a jab and a straight right before the place closed, my left hook left wondering what it could have been.

The trainer held up the pads. "One, two!" he demonstrated showing a jab and a straight right. I snapped my left and threw a hard right hand. He nodded in approval. I did it again. And again. For 20 seconds I thought there was a good chance I may have a career as a professional kick boxer. I was a potential superstar in the making. It took a trip across the world but I had found my true calling. My hands were lightning, I moved like a prime Muhammad Ali. Every punch was harder than the last. In a week I'd have my first fight. In a month I'd be in the stadiums.

And then he kicked me.

I had forgotten that kicking was in fact a part of kick boxing. My legs swept out from underneath me and I crumpled to the mat. "Don't forget leg!" he said.

I got back up. I remembered how tired I was, that it was a billion degrees outside and even hotter in the non-air-conditioned room, and that I had eaten seven pounds of bacon an hour and a half before.

I nodded to my trainer and we started again. I threw my one-two and, knowing the kick was coming, dodged out of the way. I was onto his moves. Maybe I could be a fighter after all. Maybe there was hope for me to be the first white Muay Thai kickboxing champ to come from Nova Scotia and rise to worldwide fame. As I dodged the kick, he threw a left hook at my head, stopping millimetres before connecting on my temple. "Don't forget hands!" he said like a parent reminding a kid to eat their vegetables.

As soon as I caught on to one thing, he was there with another. Dodge a hook, he'd sweep my legs with his other foot. Dodge a kick, get punched in the stomach. Soon the elbows and knees started to come. It was a blitzkrieg of unexpected limbs coming at an out of shape Canadian in a flurry.

That's how the rest of the day went. I'd catch onto something and then he'd come at me with some completely unexpected move that would leave my brain baffled. It was humbling, exciting and frustrating all at the same time. I was a complete beginner, starting from scratch at the very bottom. And that was beautiful. That's something I hadn't done in a long, long time. Everything I do now I've been doing for years. I continually push myself to improve, to be better than I was the day before. Jumping into something as a brand-new student felt so freeing. There was so much I didn't know and that was fine. I didn't have to know everything. I didn't have to put in the countless hours to try to be my best. I could just be a slow, confused, dripping-wet newbie and that was enough. That's what I was supposed to be.

After the session I laid on the mat side by side with my new trainer. I was soaked and exhausted. I closed my eyes and took deep breaths. I thought of the history in the ring I lay in. Fighters I never heard of would have pushed themselves to the edge of human capacity. They would have tested the farthest limits of will and persistence. I thought of broken bones, concussions, sweat, and blood. I thought of those who would have rose from poverty and those who's dreams would have been crushed with a flurry of limbs just a little too fast.

The history surrounded me and for a moment, I felt a part of it too.

I felt a tapping on my stomach and opened my eyes. The trainer was pointing out my "North American Mid-Section Weight."

"No more burger," he said and smiled.

I started to laugh. "No more burger," I said and nodded.

The Things He Does for Strangers:

Love Story #7

One evening in Nai Yang, Thailand, we were walking the beach board-walk eating Taylor Swift bars when Mike spotted a young girl in a wheelchair. She and a friend were parked at the edge of the boardwalk as though it was a cliff overlooking a pool of lava. It was clear a dilemma had presented itself. While we had grown accustomed to the ease of sunset strolls along the beach, this leisure was not available to everyone who visited oceanside communities. There was no one else around aside from a group of young people playing volleyball in the distance. The girls wanted to go onto the beach, but moving a steel rimmed wheelchair through the sand would be near impossible.

Mike jogged over to the girls. Realizing they didn't share a common language, he gestured to himself and then to the beach, "I'm going to take you over there" was how I interpreted his miming. The young girls exchanged looks and then smiles as Mike quickly took off, pushing the chair through the uneven terrain. Walking through sand is squishy and unstable at the best of times. Navigating a heavy, awkward, metal chair that wasn't designed for this soft terrain would surely become a train-ing technique for Rocky and Jessica Jones. The stationary wheels aching for flat ground, combatted gritty sand and unexpected seashells. Mike pushed the girl a solid 200 metres so she could be with her friend in the perfect place by the water's edge. In the light reflected by the ocean's surf, she glowed.

I stood smiling, holding Mike's dripping T-Swift ice cream, as he jogged back towards me. We spent the evening writing our names in the sand and watching the shimmering sunset—the things most people now take pictures of for Instagram. But at this time in our past, such self-indulgences were yet to take over travel experiences. We were present. I relished in sharing these days with my love. To see him in his element. To see him go out of his way at every opportunity to try and make the world a better place. To see him unquestionably offer a lending hand to someone he had never met and never would again.

That's the kind of thing he does for strangers.

You can only imagine the things he does for me.

If you can travel with someone like this, you're assured a lifetime of magnificent memories.

BERT VS. ERNIE

On Phi Phi Island we came across a bar with a kickboxing ring in the centre. Drunken tourists could enter the ring to fight professional kick boxers. It was by far the greatest thing I'd ever come across. I'm typically not very assertive in my desires to partake in certain events, but with this I was putting my foot down. We WERE going to this bar EVERY NIGHT we were here and there was nothing Kristen could do about it. Of the thousands of clothing stores, jewelry shops, petting zoos, gemstone dispensaries, gardens and shoe stores I entered without hesitation, I had earned a few nights at this bar watching dumb Americans get their faces punched in.

Inside you could sit ringside with giant glasses of Tiger beer while people voluntarily got in the ring with legitimate killers. Every fight basically went the same: the drunken moron would enter the ring smiling and laughing and go in swinging at a chiseled statue of a man who would dodge everything with the gracefulness and ease of Bruce Lee fighting a baby. The assassin would throw a few "playful" kicks and punches at the moron to see how they'd react. The moron would try one last ditch effort to land a shot and the Goliath would hit them once in the ribs with a kick or punch at about 25 per cent his capacity. The moron would drop and writhe in pain and give a "no more" type gesture to call an end to it. The Goliath would pick up the squirming moron and everyone would cheer.

The second type of fight was when two morons from the crowd would fight each other. An old Thai man would stand in the ring and point to people in the crowd. "You . . . Fight!" Once one person agreed, he'd either keep pointing at people until he found someone, or someone volunteered.

I knew something like this could never happen anywhere else in the world so I was fascinated. I saw a drunk, 20-year-old American girl break her leg within ten seconds and fall to the mat, screaming in agony. I couldn't believe how many people were willing to get into the ring in a foreign country and fight a full-contact sport against a stranger. I sat beside a tall, D-1 basketball player from the states who the old man in the ring tried to get me to fight. Maybe we just weren't drunk enough, but both of us adamantly shook our heads with a definitive "not a chance." For all I knew he could have been a golden-gloves boxer, and for all he knew I could have trained for one day in Chiang Mai and sweat so much my pores began to drown. We both nodded at each other with a mutual respect.

At one point in the bar, a group of Asian guys came up to Kristen and pointed at their camera. "You want me to take your picture? Sure!" She said. The spokesperson for the group, the one with the camera, shook his head and pointed at her. He made the motion of taking a picture. "I think he wants to take a picture of you," I said. Kristen pointed to herself. "Me?"

He nodded. The three guys were friendly and seemed nice enough. Kristen just shrugged her shoulders and told them sure. She sat there and the man with the camera took a quick shot. He gave a thumbs up and smiled. Kristen felt like a celebrity. A half hour later, a server at the bar came over with a giant plate of chicken fingers for us. We told him we didn't order anything. He pointed to the buds from the photo session who smiled and gave some more thumbs ups. All Kristen had to do was let them take a picture and we got a free plate of chicken fingers. It was a top 10 moment for sure. If it was *that* easy, what else could we do? What other ways could Kristen use her looks to get food or make money? I realized that if things ever got bad we could always count on Kristen's blonde hair and smile to get us through.

On a Monday night, we sat with probably 20 other people in the bar. I sat ringside with my litre glass of beer, watching morons beat the piss out of each other, and plowing back chicken fingers that were bought for us because my wife's pretty. After one particular match that ended with a tattoo covered Brit losing to a guy on an acid trip, two Thai fighters entered the ring for an exhibition.

They were probably 18 or 19. One guy was long and lean and the other guy stockier. Sinewy muscle bulged on both of their bodies. I watched them enter the ring poised and with purpose. In proper Thai kick-boxing matches, there's a ritual of song, movement and dance before each fight. As the two combatants performed these sacred movements, I looked around the bar. People sat at their tables engaged in conversation and drinks. Young guys in tank tops with white teeth and perfect tans tried their damned hardest to work their magic on any girl in sight.

The music ended and they started to fight. They circled towards each other slowly, with caution. They threw some light kicks and punches, feeling each other out. After a few minutes of this, the stocky guy threw a vicious head-kick that landed with full impact on the lankier guy's temple (I don't know what either of their names were, so I'll refer to the stockier gentleman as Bert and the lankier fighter as Ernie).

Bert's shin smashed across Ernie's face like a baseball bat. I jumped in my seat. I'd never seen a person get hit like that in my entire life. The force of that kick could easily kill someone. It was worse than a car accident. He went down. "He's dead!" I yelled out. He got up immediately and rocketed forward. He threw a flurry of swift combinations at Bert, his hands a blur of speed and precision. He blasted Bert with an earthquake like knee to the face. It went back and forth like this the entire time. An all-out war. Ernie kicked Bert through the ropes and into the crowd at one point. He came back in, limping, probably a sprained or broken ankle. Both were bleeding. Their limbs were trained from a young age to do this with precision. They were lighting fast and tactical, every movement calculated and graceful. They clinched and kneed each other in the faces, kicked their shins till they were bruised and swollen. I'd never seen anything like it. They were magicians of violence, without a doubt the toughest and best athletes I'd ever seen. And they beat the hell out of each other for our entertainment.

Black eyes began to swell and blood dripped from the fighter's noses. I looked around the bar. The guys in tank tops were talking to the girls in skirts. No one cared about the war in front of them.

I sat there thinking over my beer and chicken fingers. I had travelled 13,918 kilometers to get there. I had taken planes, buses, taxis, and boats. I could travel the world and sit in a bar with other people like me, each of us with everything we need to be comfortable: cold water bottles in front of us, enough money in our pockets to buy booze and food, a hotel to go back to. I felt an incredible surge of guilt rush over me. Were we were exploiting them? Were we just wealthy tourists taking advantage of two guys fighting their hearts out to make us happy?

Bert and Ernie gave every ounce of what they could to an uninterested crowd. I was mesmerized. They were so fast, so graceful, and brave. They could have annihilated a prime Mike Tyson. I felt like I was witnessing something monumental, something that would change the course of the universe we inhabit. The fight ended and Bert and Ernie simply walked out of the ring. There was no winner because it was just for our entertainment. I sat there speechless. I didn't know what to say or how to move forward. I felt like I was doing something wrong, like their bruises were because of me and the people around me.

As two more morons got into the ring to try and impress their friends and the girls they'd been hitting on, I saw Bert and Ernie walking through the crowd with their hands out looking for money. They just put on a better fight than any $50 Pay Per View I'd ever watched and were asking the crowd for loose change. Most people shook their heads, some not even bothering to look in their direction to acknowledge them.

They deserved so much more. They deserved whatever they've ever wanted.

When they came by, I took out all the money I had in my pockets and handed to them. But it wasn't enough. It would never be enough. What they just did was worth more than everything I could ever offer them. They bowed and thanked me profusely before moving on.

They made their way through the crowd. Maybe they'd make enough money for a meal, a couple drinks or to buy *Terminator 2* on DVD. I sat there in silence, the morons in the ring winning the audience over with their graceless battle.

Airport Adventures

We often hear, "I like travelling but I don't like airports." We understand. You have to deal with the classic frustrations: line-ups, stale air, security, and overpriced sandwiches topped with question-able meat and mayonnaise-wet bread. But beyond that, you also find kids gleefully pulling their polka-dot suitcases and people-watching that rivals "Wal-Mart meets a small-town doctor's office."

Despite experiencing every airport nightmare since the construction of Hounslow Heath, we still enjoy this part of the travel ritual. Airports mark the beginning of an unknown adventure. They're the spark before the smoke. They're the gateway that can make two misfits who came from nothing believe in possibility; to be fearless, to believe that their humble beginnings were their superpower rather than their barricade.

I once stayed overnight at the San Jose airport in Costa Rica. I was woken at 4 a.m. by a mob of attractive men in suits, each of them carrying a matching duffle bag. It was the national football team filming an Adidas commercial and yes, it was worth being sprawled out on a bench the size of a laptop for eight hours just to catch a glimpse of.

There are silver linings every so often, and we like to find them. Eventually, you learn both tricks and tolerances that promise an enjoyable experience. You learn airports can be the amusing movie previews before the Oscar winning main event.

Enjoying airports simply takes a bit of preparation.

TRAVEL TIPS:

1. Always check-in to your flight the moment you are permitted. If that means setting an alarm for the wee hours in the morning or

interrupting dinner on your last night of vacation, do it anyway. Reserving your seat in advance and knowing your name is in a system somewhere is like checking the stove is off before leaving the house. It's peace of mind.

2. Travel with carry-on only. I know some of you have a list of reasons why this isn't possible. I stand by my advice. Leave the "shoe bag" behind. The number of times I've gotten on a plane before another passenger is in direct correlation to my scarce luggage. Debbie and her three-piece Gucci bags and matching chihuahua is not getting home to Dallas anytime soon. Kristen with her grimy shirt and pair of black sneakers she argues go with everything will be landing in Halifax shortly.

3. Bring a reusable water bottle and fill it at every opportunity. Disposable bottles are so 1995 and dehydration will only make your jet lag worse. More importantly, the tablespoon of water you're offered on the plane is barely enough to swallow a Gravol.

4. Pack a food bag. We always carry one (that can double as just an extra bag when you arrive at your destination) filled with trail mix, PB sammies, gum, chocolate, etc. Not only will you avoid buying $18 questionable meat and wet bread, but it helps pass the time having snacks to indulge in. Make sure you throw them away before leaving the plane. Near-arrests at customs and declarations have taught us it's better to leave the two bites of your meatball sub on the plane than try to smuggle a midnight snack onwards.

5. Download the app for your airline. You'll have access to movies, flight changes and boarding passes at your fingertips. It takes five minutes and you might get to watch *Legally Blonde 3*.

6. ARRIVE EARLY. I can't stress this one enough. Most airports say an hour early for domestic and two hours for international. We usually tack an extra hour onto this. If anything goes wrong with customs, security or line-ups, one less thing we have to stress about

is running late. Worst-case scenario is everything goes smooth and we have extra time for a drink or people-watching.

These tips don't come with any guarantees. If it's a blizzard outside and your flights are delayed, you won't give a fuck about your water bottle. But imagine if there's bad weather *and* you're thirsty. Even then it can make a small difference. Good old patience, understanding, and acknowledgement that, "you're lucky you get to travel at all" has to kick in during airport dilemmas. This is often the space we occupy and how many of our airport stories came to be.

Canada: Toronto to Prague, "Running to make a connection"

While you can (mostly) manage what time you arrive at an airport by land, arriving via air for a connecting flight is a gamble. It's a whole new level of relinquishing control. You're left hopeful that the weather will be great, the plane won't have any structural problems, birds stay out of the propellors and no one lights up a dart in the bathroom, all of which could cause delays.

Our connection to Prague was departing Pearson airport in 12 minutes when our plane hit the tarmac. In this situation, your body feels like a combination of having the flu and public speaking. You're trying to be calm and normal. You may even smile and make light of the stressful timeline, though you've already managed to let the entire crew and cabin full of passengers know you have ONLY 12 MINUTES TO MAKE YOUR CONNECTION!

"It's not like we're going to Montreal or something afterwards either. We'd have to wait 24 hours if we don't get on this flight for the next one. We'll just have to make a run for it," I rambled on with a quiver in my voice, panic revealing itself in the form of sweat stains and red neck blotches. I hated every other human on the plane. They were slow, oblivious barriers between me and the exit. It took 1,000 years for the seat-belt light to illuminate, signalling it was time to get off the plane. I body bombed everything in my path disembarking and Usain Bolt-ed my way to wherever the hell gate 24C was.

In this instance, gate 24C was about 800 meters away and we had just over three minutes to get there. Now, we're no Olympians, but we're in okay shape for a couple of almost 40-year-olds. We go for walks every day, throw in some strength and HIIT routines, and regularly follow Boho Beautiful yoga (note: if you want your partners to start doing yoga, Juliana from BB should seal the deal. She looks like "Spiritual Barbie" and her voice sounds like a back rub feels), but this time crunch was asking for a record I wasn't sure I was built to give. With our loaded packs and determination, we took off on a sprint that would surely land us roles in the next Marvel movie. Darting between bystanders and navigating golf carts carrying old people, I started to feel the acidy whisper of vomit rising from my stomach. In a split second I had gone from three hours of statue-sitting on an airplane to the fastest capable speed my body was able to achieve. With about 150 metres left to go, Mike took the lead. I thought I would die. I yelled, "I'm gonna die!" and Mike turned his head halfway around. "We got this! We're almost there!"

We were obviously the last two people to get on the flight. We were drenched in airport scuzz, I had just swallowed my own bile, we didn't have time to pee or fill up on water, and somewhere amidst this debacle, I managed to break my glasses. But! We made our flight . . .

Thailand: Phuket to Chiang Mai, "The facial lady"

People-watching is a weird human behaviour that we all have in common but try desperately to hide. You strategically go out of your way to remain unnoticed by the subject of your observations. Wouldn't it be easier if we could all just accept that we're staring each other down? We ARE passing judgment and filling in the gaps of other people's entire life history for the sake of our own entertainment. That happens to everyone, at all times, in airports.

If you get really lucky, you'll have the opportunity for some real story worthy sightings: the Costa Rican soccer team with their Amazon muscles is just one example. We've also seen a family of four who we named "the glasses family," all of whom would have looked identical without glasses but happened to also be wearing matching glasses. It was weird that even the parents looked alike. We've seen women with Botoxed eyes complemented by thigh high boots, and new mothers with black-circled eyes and Ugg boots. There was the hippie guy trying to assemble a vegan leather hammock who smelled like patchouli and was reading either *The Celestine Prophecy* or *Siddhartha* while twirling the beads in his dreadlocks. And in Thailand, there was the middle-aged woman who gave herself a facial and then ate a bag of cotton balls while sitting across from us at the boarding gate.

She was probably in her 60s and was accompanied by both a male companion and half a dozen large canvas bags. The bags were filled with boxes. The boxes were filled with thick, white, glue-like cream. Maybe it was rhino semen or whipped ivory tusk. Maybe she would eat some and suddenly look 25 again. I was giddy with anticipation. There are endless traditions that Eastern medicine practices. We would get to witness a healing session right here in the Phuket airport. My curiosity was inappropriately high. My eyes fixed on the jars like a magnet to steel.

There's a technique to watching someone without them realizing. With our eyes like subtle lasers and smirks barely contained, we take things out of our bags as though we're discussing them, but we're actually losing it over what we're witnessing in the seats across from us. This allows us to discuss our observations in mutual amusement while appearing as though we're simply double checking we've packed warm clothes. Maybe she *did* know I was watching, but I like to think we have a sneaky way of staring someone down without them noticing.

The woman dipped all four fingers into a jar, the white goo spilling out onto the palm of her hand. She placed her second hand over top of the first into a prayer position and gently spread the mayonnaise-like goo between her hands as though the world's most decadent bologna sandwich were being crafted. She lifted her sandwich hands towards her face and covered every inch of her wrinkles and facial features. The goo jiggled and slid around on her face. She was a lemon meringue pie.

Her husband sat silently, unflinching, reading his newspaper the entire time . . .

She was sitting directly across from us. If she and I both lifted our legs, our feet would touch. I wondered what was so great about this cream it had to be applied *right now*, in the middle of an airport, 20 minutes before boarding a flight. Lotion is one thing, but this was a mask thick as a Mars bar. She left the glue-cream on until it started to slide down her neck. Her partner did not so much as look towards her. They sat in complete comfort, almost boredom, as she executed her mini spa day in the busiest, loudest, most non-private venue that exists. I sat in awe as the Thai woman moved onto the next phase of her ritual. Reaching into her purse this time, she pulled out a pearly white, rounded cotton ball. It's possible it was something else. A Thai marshmallow perhaps, but with its wispy white hairs and shiny gleam, I'm comfortable proclaiming: it was a cotton ball. I dwell on this identification because the ball went straight from the mystery purse into the woman's mouth, likely soaking up some of the glue cream from her face on the way.

The facial lady just ate a cotton ball.

She just consumed spun fabric while buried beneath a meringue topped face in the middle of a crowded airport.

I questioned my own sense of self-confidence. I was much more aghast than she about what had just happened. I figured it was a superstition or cultural practice I had yet to encounter. Pie face and cotton ball candy before flying was not outlined in any of the travel guides *I* had read, but embracing new discoveries always was.

SUNSETS:

Love Story #8

We sat at the water's edge on a beach in Koh Samet. The warm waves lapped calmly at our feet, trying their hardest to claim our sandals and make the ocean their new home. The stars felt a little bit different in Thailand. They all looked a little red, as though we were surrounded by a sky full of infinite Mars'. The moon sat high above us, patient, still, and demanding every bit of our attention. It was only a half moon but still as bright as any I'd seen before then. Her face was lit up and she looked every bit as beautiful as she did in all my best dreams. Because that's what it all was: my best dream, everything I could ever want come true. Her skin was getting darker. Soon she wouldn't burn. Soon the remarkably hot Thailand sun would have no power over her. Soon the tan lines from the three different bikinis she bought would all mould into a dark, summer glow. She was, at that moment, what every man in the world hopes to hell he comes across at some point in his life. I held her hand, the waves lapping, the moon glowing and all those red planets above us.

A HALF-ASSED VIEW
OF NEW YORK

New York City is the opposite of where I grew up. It's energetic, bold, iconic and overflowing with personality. My hometown was slow, quiet, familiar and was populated with more cows than people. The contrast is what makes landing in New York so exhilarating. You feel like your blood is oxygenated and saturated with every multi-vitamin ever made. You feel capable of achieving dreams and being the person you always wanted to be.

I wondered if the man we saw on Fifth Avenue was the person he always wanted to be.

He was wearing a tailored tweed suit jacket, complete with starched white shirt and perfectly knotted tie. He carried a brown leather briefcase with shiny bronze buckles and leather shoes that were yet to be broken in. His hair was slicked back and face freshly shaved. He walked with confidence and class which complemented his distinguished swagger. He embodied New York City. His stature and presence represented what it was like to "make it." He looked as though he belonged, maybe even owned, the office building he was on his way to.

There was just one thing.

He did not have any pants on.

The man walked with his head held higher than the Chrysler building, his white gleaming butt cheeks hanging out from under the hem of his starched Prada dress shirt, along with any sense of shame that still remained. People looked but didn't stare. This was normal in New York.

This was what made the city special in our eyes. You could be anybody. This guy was 99 per cent ideal man, one per cent naked bum.

Mike and I were 100 per cent kids on Christmas morning who had just been gifted a unicorn and Willy Wonka's candy factory. In true New York fashion, the city had delivered, leaving nothing behind.

MICHAEL JACKSON:

What I'd Do if Born Elsewhere

As we travel to different parts of the world, we're fortunate to be exposed to a large and varying degree of people, their culture, and general way of life. We've eaten weird bugs, rode in ox carts, meditated in temples, and let random strangers on the street poke and prod us so they could feel first-hand what a thirtysomething-kind-of-chubby-and-out-of-shape-white-person's stomach feels like.

One thing that we're exposed to around every corner in the places we've been is the way that people make a living. Around the world, everyone has to survive—one way or another. Sometimes I wonder what I'd do if I was born elsewhere, if I didn't grow up in a middle-class family in rural Nova Scotia. My parents didn't have much money, but I always ate. I always got to hockey practice. I was *usually* warm (one of the reasons we could afford hockey practice was Dad's stringent monitoring of the thermostat with sniper-like focus combined with a thriftiness historians in apocalyptical times will recall as a Bible for survival. I'll take a cold nose in the middle of the night for slap shots and top-shelf goals any day). I was from an average family with three kids who lived in an average house, drank six litres of milk a day, had a cat named Spike, drove around in a shitty car that shook and sounded like an earthquake, and at Christmas I got a present that wasn't awesome but was better than a lump of coal and kick in the nuts. We could get by in North America and were better off than 95 per cent of the rest of the world.

I'd like to think that no matter where I grew up I'd get to follow my dream. But I know that's not the case. Opportunities aren't equal, and I've been fortunate. If I was born in any of the places I travelled to, I'd with certainty be living a much different life. What if I was born in Latin America? Would I sell extraordinarily long USB cables on the streets of San Jose? Would I be a pushy water salesman, or balance a ridiculous amount of hats on my head in hopes of impressing some passerby for a quick sale? There's always the option to sell sunglasses, shine shoes, drive a taxi, or wholesale giant edible ants as an aphrodisiac and walk around holding a sign that reads "Big Ass Ants." That wouldn't be so bad. I'd be out and about all day, getting exercise and conversing with new people. And I suppose I could dip into my miracle product any time I wanted.

If I was born in Thailand I'd probably end up being a kick-boxer. I'm long and (used to be) lean. I'd be the perfect build for it. I'd get my face beat in at a bar in the middle of nowhere for pennies. Maybe I'd be a drug dealer like Bobby in Phi Phi. I'd pose as a fruit salesman but really have a stash of the good stuff inside a secret hidden coconut. I'm generally friendly and love striking up a good conversation. I think I'd be a great drug dealer.

Kristen would probably sell art on the side of the road or give foot massages in Bangkok. She'd be one of the thousands we passed yelling "Massaaaage" in a thick Thai accent that every traveller who's ever visited the country can easily duplicate. Dad would be the guy that carries heavy tables. That's a real job. I saw the same guy do it daily in Cartagena—just lifting 100-pound tables back and forth all day as your arms get big and knees wear down. Mom would probably balance food on her head, wear a colourful dress and charge 1,000 pesos for a photo with her. Everyone likes Mom; she'd do pretty good.

Maybe I would have been one of the lucky ones. Maybe I would have gone to school and learned math. I'd work a good job for the government, own a home, and have all I need. But I know how lucky I really am. I know that I've been born into circumstances that most people around the world only dream of.

Whatever it is I imagine, I know that I'd end up like the Michael Jackson impersonator—awkwardly dancing with stiff limbs, hitting falsetto notes as drunk American kids in their 20s laugh at my pseudo moves. But I'd fucking go for it. I wouldn't hold back. I'd be dressed in a shitty suit, doing shitty imitation MJ moves and singing high notes with all my guts hoping to impress the endless sea of Caucasian faces passing me by; a perpetual gold rush I can never really tap fully into. And as the college kids walk away, I'd hear one of them mouth, "He's actually pretty good," as he throws 50 cents out of his trust fund into my top hat on the sidewalk in front of me.

At the end of the day, everyone's just trying to get by, pay rent, eat a few meals a day, afford a drink on Friday, and maybe a present for their lover. However we have to do it may differ from place to place, but we're all in the same boat—and would likely be on a drastically different one if we grew up elsewhere.

FIVE-STAR HOTEL

One of the biggest barriers to travel is the expense. Mike and I both grew up in humble, rural Nova Scotian households where cutting coupons and getting yelled at for taking showers longer than five minutes shaped our childhoods. I hauled water every summer until I was a teenager because our well would run dry, and instant potatoes were a suppertime staple. Despite all that, our parents always offered us what adventure they could.

Family travel usually meant going camping in a mouldy tent or driving to the closest urban centre to eat at an all-you-can-eat buffet. This didn't bother me growing up, but my adventurous spirit was constantly flapping her wild wings. Once I started *really* travelling, it quickly became one of the most important aspects of my life. It's what made me light up with joy and feel connected to myself and others. For many years, I could only afford cheap hostels or shitty motels. In Central America, you could often find a place for just a few dollars a night. That budget promised you some accompanying bed bugs or rats, but I never cared. I was away!

Fast-forward to my 30s when my bank account was slightly larger and my tolerance for rodents slightly smaller. I curiously looked up a five-star hotel in Bangkok where we would be wrapping up a month of travel. The country was known for affordable everything, so it was worth exploring accommodation choices.

For $60 we could stay in a Hilton Hotel suite outfitted with a king-sized bed, washer and dryer, whirlpool tub, and buffet breakfast. I couldn't believe it. My travel life changed with this knowledge and I booked us in for our last night away in the castle of luxury.

The 30-some days leading up to the night in the Hilton was primarily spent in $20 hotel rooms. No rats, but no Egyptian cotton either. Our appearance was what you might expect after a month spent on buses, full-moon parties, red-light districts, beaches filled with drug dealers and surviving on $1.50 mango salad. We were smelly, rugged Canadians who were constantly sweating and always looked lost. When we arrived at the Hilton, it was as though two skunks had just landed at the spa.

Nevertheless, we were treated like William and Kate on their wedding day. A procession of Thai men and women lined up on either side of us, bowing relentlessly as we walked from the sliding glass doors to the main counter. We were handed fresh squeezed juice and smiled at like we had just entered heaven. Every time we spoke, someone else would bow at us, their abdominals clearly made of titanium steel. It was confusing because we looked like two PIGDOGS who had been pulled from the sewer, but we liked the attention. I had continuously cut the dirty bottoms of my pants shorter to "clean" them and Mike's beard looked like a scouring pad in a Nicaraguan prison. But Thai hospitality saw no threshold of disgust. For 60 bucks, we were worshipped like warriors back from battle. If there's money worth spending, it's on the opportunity, maybe the *only* opportunity, to walk into a place as disgusting strangers and walk out as reinvented royalty. We relished in the satin sheets and washed weeks' worth of insect poison and risky decisions from our skin. We tightened our toes on the plush carpets, gripping the expensive fibres between our sparkling limbs and turned our tattered rags of clothing into cloaks fit for Buddha himself. It was a rare indulgence that we toasted by clinking our flutes of coconut water and snuggling in our billowing bath robes. Five stars shone down from the heavens unto our childhood disbeliefs.

WHAT WE NEEDED AND WHERE WE NEEDED TO BE

Travelling can be tiring. When you're constantly in transit, switching between different forms of transportation, lugging heavy backpacks, eating weird foods, sleeping in different beds, and drinking more than you normally do, it can wear you down.

The newness keeps you energized. The adrenalin from seeing a place you've never been keeps your blood filled with all the feel-good chemicals you need. And that's really the point of it all. To let those new places and experiences fill you up with enough good to keep you sane and upright for a little longer.

We drove into the city of Medellin in a shuttle. Everything was lush, green and vibrant. All we knew about the city was that it was at one point—when Pablo Escobar and the boys were going hard in the paint on the cocaine exporting—the most dangerous city in the world. Now, according to one site we looked at online, it was moderately safe and had won an award for innovation. While my dad assumed gunfire around every corner and was waiting for the inevitable phone call detailing our capture and enslavement at the hands of a violent rebel militia cutting off our various body parts to sell for witchcraft potions on the black market, we were excited to explore the growing metropolis.

The city is essentially in a valley surrounded by the Andes Mountains. When we started to descend, we looked down upon the endless city sprawl and the mesmerizing beauty of the encircling mountain range. Every turn was a new view filling us up with endorphins. The juxtaposition of the city and its towering hills was beautiful. We bolted down the steep slope, not sure if we wanted to go slower to see the view or faster to get to our destination and experience it. That excitement is what we live for. It's the early stages of falling for someone, your birthday, getting what you fought hard for, a passionate night with your celebrity crush. Life is meant for those moments to take place as often as they can. Sometimes they're few and far between. Sometimes the pressures of the world build up so much that we think we can't feel them anymore. Winding down that road overlooking it all, everything was right. It was exactly what we needed and where we needed to be.

PETER'S HISTORY LESSON:
Medellin Walking Tour

W e've learned one of the best ways to get acquainted with a new
city is to take a guided walking tour. The first time we did this
was in Prague and, while I admit it felt a little "old people" for our liking,
we wound up learning so much about the city's history and folklore that
we've been doing them ever since. Walking tours are typically pay what
you can and are organized to balance both scheduled activities and personal leisure time. You meet other travellers from across the globe and
sometimes access places you couldn't on your own. The guides are usually
bilingual and always enthusiastic.

With a story like that of Medellin's history, a day tour quickly becomes
a juicy true crime novel. Pablo Escobar ensured this legacy. I couldn't
imagine visiting Colombia without at least a curiosity about cocaine and
cartels. We knew a guided tour of the city would surely include some of
each and were equally looking forward to learning something new, such as
who invented the Chicken Glove? It was when we called concierge asking
what the best Pablo Escobar tour was that we faced a humbling lesson.

The Medellin drug cartel reigned supreme from the early '70s to the
early '90s. Their power and influence created an insurmountable threat.
When things happen far enough from home, they feel unrelatable, making
it easy to overlook the ugly truth of it all. This single organized crime
group smuggled and sold up to 60 million dollars' worth of cocaine A
DAY. They killed and kidnapped thousands of people and executed political figures including a minister of justice, a supreme court judge and two

federal DEA agents. Every person in this city has been scarred by this part of their nation's history, including our concierge.

"We don't offer tours, or work with companies who do, on that topic."

In an instant, we felt like the world's worst tourists. World's worst *people*. We later learned that the locals didn't even say "his" name. Pablo Escobar was but a nightmare from the nation's past.

We quickly changed course and started researching alternative tours. It was valuable insight for us to have experienced early on in our travels, "DON'T TALK ABOUT COCAINE IN THE COCAINE CAPITAL OF THE WORLD." We found a trusty pay what you can walking tour that advertised as a half-day guided adventure around various parts of the city where you would see art, taste food, and explore off-the-beaten track attractions. It sounded perfect.

A short train ride away, we met a group of about 20 people from around the globe who just so happened to also be in Colombia, on that day, at that time, for this tour. Our guide was in his early 40s but had the energy of a teenager. He assembled us on a set of stairs, facing him like the audience that we were. Spanning the group, we introduced ourselves and where we were from. Other than Mike, I didn't remember anyone's name, including our guide's, but it's a friendly way to start the tour and I pretended to pay attention to the collection of voices shouting out where they were from. I'm terrible at remembering names and am an avid supporter of name tags for this reason. I'm embarrassingly one of those people who forgets your name the moment it leaves your lips. I've tried using tricks like repeating it three times or associating with something memorable (Susan likes seaweed) but it's just something I struggle with. I think this is why when all 20 of us had completed our introductions, I was astounded that our guide, one-by-one, pointed us out and identified us with precision. He had just memorized all 20 of our foreign names, having heard them just once in addition to whatever trivial fact we opted to share with the strangers that surrounded us. He didn't forget or mispronounce a single one. I knew he would be an exceptional guide and that no matter what we learned about Medellin sculptures, inventors, or drug dealers, it would pale in comparison to the memory magician who stood before us.

Because I don't possess either the courtesy or capacity to remember his name (I'm not proud of this), let's call our guide Peter.

Peter shared that he was born and raised in Colombia but in his early adulthood attended university in New York City. He earned a PhD (damned if I remember what in) and later worked at a news station. Or maybe it was a theatre company? What I DO remember is the part when he told us that he went from being a professor at NYU to being a pay what you can tour guide in Colombia because he felt he owed it to his people and his culture. This kind of pride is unforgettable. He had sacrificed our idea of a better life for one of financial instability and lesser status with the intent to revive Colombia's reputation. Peter was once again my hero. While Pablo's name had been banished, it was people like Peter who were sharing the other side of Medellin's story. A story of people helping each other. A story of endurance, strength, and patriotism. He told us that at one point in their city's history, you wouldn't leave for groceries without kissing your loved ones goodbye. There was too great a chance of getting shot on the way and never making it home again. He told us that everyone had *at least* an uncle who had been impacted by the cartel. Now the emphasis of the people was on rebuilding and showcasing other points of pride, such as their award-winning transportation system, export sector, and accommodating tourist industry. Desperate to forget, the people of Medellin have made it their mission to highlight and celebrate their culture. Their hospitality, green spaces, trendy neighbourhoods and progressive outlook made this one of our favourite cities we've ever visited.

We spent all morning walking main roads and back alleys. Peter led us down streets filled with vendors and cafes selling fresh breads and pastries. We learned about the coffee trade and visited a live plant wall that climbed the pillars of an elevated highway. We learned about the barrios where poverty was your destiny and gave reason for a history of crime. We saw endless street graffiti and hipster venues. The city had everything your favourite city would and learning about it from a man with this level of knowledge and passion was thrilling. An NYU professor was teaching us about his home while escorting us, by name, throughout. All for "whatever you could afford that day."

Peter ended the tour with showing us works from Colombian sculpture Fernando Botero, who has donated more than 20 large, bronze sculptures to the city. Botero's most famous works include *The Birds of Peace:* two oversized, plump birds that sit side-by-side in the gritty San Antonio Plaza. The original single bird statue, built in 1995, was blown to pieces at an outdoor concert by terrorist groups. In June of that year, 22 pounds of dynamite was left at the base of the statue, and upon exploding killed 30 and injured more than 200 innocent bystanders. The leftist guerrilla group Revolutionary Armed Forces of Colombia (better known by the Spanish acronym, FARC) took responsibility for the bombing and claimed it was a message aimed at Colombia's then-defence minister Fernando Botero Zea. He was Fernando Botero's son. In 2000, Botero donated an identical, undamaged bronze bird. He insisted that the exploded statue remain in the plaza. It has since been carved with the names of the bombing victims and situated beside the second sculpture, symbolizing the juxtaposition of the city's then and now.

Two identical birds, two opposite representations.

The city voted to keep both statues as a means of acknowledging their conflicted and painful past and also celebrating their durable future. It was a powerful way to end the tour and it connected to the people and the place. We left feeling impressed by Colombia and her ability to move on. We left feeling grateful for how humanity always chooses resilience.

OPEN MIKE:

True Love

Since I was 13, the longest I'd ever gone without playing guitar was probably four days. I don't really consider it an instrument anymore; it's more just another part of me. Something always within reach, something my mind and body need to noodle around on to feel normal. I've never once thought, "I need to play guitar now"; it's more a necessity that happens autonomically, a part of who and what I am.

I didn't think about it before we left, but in Thailand I'd be going without a guitar for a long, long time. Being in a completely foreign place with different cultures and new experiences can certainly help ease the burden of being without a part of your lifeblood. But it doesn't eliminate it.

By week three I felt like the end of the movie *Requiem for a Dream* was happening to my innards. I needed my fix. If it was a cheap Yamaha or even an Ovation I didn't care. I needed to strum chords, to let my mind fall completely into the trance of sounds and potential ideas.

When we arrived in Pai, we rented scooters and adventured around the countryside, watched the most miraculous lightning storm you'd ever see light up a giant white Buddha on the mountainside from our hotel, and at night sat in the town and watched as the ever-changing movie of people fluttered by.

Walking around one evening I heard it in the distance: an incredibly shitty version of "Summer of '69." The timing wavered like an about to implode record player and the voice sounded like a dying penguin. It was the most beautiful thing I'd ever heard. I knew instantly that it was an open mic. No professional musician would ever sing a song that poorly. No one could ever "gig" performing like that. It was undeniably an open mic where a guy with a hat on sideways from Des Moines, Iowa, who thinks he's Mick Jagger gets on stage to impress girls who have never been to a concert other than the time their cool aunt took them to see Katy Perry.

I started to run. I didn't say a word. I didn't know if Kristen was behind me or not, but I needed to follow the sounds. If she was kidnapped on the streets of Pai, so be it—we had a good run and I'd love her always.

It got louder and louder, the dying penguin squealed in my ears and my smile grew. When I got there, it was the smallest bar I'd ever seen. It was probably 10- by10-foot room that opened up onto the street. There was a guy on stage (hat on sideways) belting out the last notes of the Bryan Adams classic. There was no one else in the bar. No bartender. No patrons. Just one man and me standing directly before him. Kristen eventually caught up.

"Are you okay?!" she asked.

"Guitar," I responded.

The man held out the guitar in a "you want?" type gesture. I nodded.

I took the guitar and he got up to tend the bar. He was the host of the open mic, the bartender, and the bouncer.

I made a G chord and strummed. I could feel the life coming back into my body. "How's everybody doing out there?" I asked into the mic.

I started to play.

It felt otherworldly. My entire essence had been missing something and it was now fulfilled.

After about five songs the man walked the six inches to the stage and handed me a free beer. He made a "continuously spinning the hand in a circular like motion with index finger outstretched" gesture to indicate keep playing.

I knew what he was doing. I had done it myself. Ten years earlier, I hosted an open mic in my hometown with my friend and bandmate Andrew. We got 50 bucks each and all the booze we could drink. When you're 20 years old and part of your contract is UNLIMITED ALCOHOL, you try to consume the world's sum of it each night. Every time a performer got up, we encouraged them to play as much as they wanted. This would allow us to pound back drinks at an unhealthy, liver damaging rate. The first week we hosted, a guy a few years older than me, named Earl, got up on stage. Earl came from a tough background. His dad spent time in prison and his family never caught any breaks. I went to school with his brother and liked him but knew they didn't have it easy. Until Earl walked up to us and asked to perform, I had never once heard of him being a musician. From what I can remember, through trying to drink a liquor store's worth of booze between songs, was Earl basically being Jimi Hendrix, John Lennon, and Freddy Mercury rolled into one.

Unfortunately, no one ever paid enough attention to give reasonable feedback on his performance. The next day, I'd ask my friends: "Was Earl God on stage last night?!"

"Fuck . . . I was too drunk to remember my middle name," would be the general consensus.

Whether Earl was a rock star or poor kid sloppily plucking away at "Classical Gas" didn't matter. What mattered was that Earl would play all night. After each song, we'd just give Earl the "continuously spinning the hand in a circular like motion with index finger outstretched" gesture to encourage him to continue playing. "KEEP 'ER ROLLIN', EARL! SOUNDIN' GREAT, BUDDY!" we'd yell and order another three shots of rum.

The man wanted me to keep playing so I did. For three hours. I played every song I could. A crowd came and sang along to the covers they knew. People joined me on stage to play harmonica to Neil Young, and tried to play along with my original songs but ultimately just messed them up and made them worse. I didn't care though. I was playing again. We went back every night we were there. I played for hours, got free booze, and let the Thai Bryan Adams focus on serving drinks rather than have to try his best at "Cuts Like a Knife."

With travelling, you get to find out who you really are. You come across things that change your perspective. Your new experiences shape you into who you're meant to be. You also recognize what it is you can't change about yourself. There are things that are a part of you that aren't meant to be altered. That's a part of the process too. Deep down inside we're all something. Our blood is made up of the things that happened, the things we felt, what we saw and who we saw it with. I don't ever want to change the good parts. I'll try to make sure of that.

Tony's Sleep and the Migraine

We had spent the evening before piecing our backpacks together in preparation for our flight to San Francisco. Our travel agent had waved her magic wand (the same wand that all travel agents have, apparently) and booked us on an extended layover in San Fran at no extra cost.

> **TRAVEL TIP:** *An extended layover is a great way to add a stop to an existing itinerary. Our flight back passed through San Francisco anyway, so having the option to stick around the connecting city at no additional cost was brilliant. This quick pit stop would bridge our time between Muay Thai fighting, duck feet and near-death boat rides back into fiddle music, lobster tails, and an over-abundance of plaid soon to greet us in Nova Scotia.*

Before we left Bangkok, we were reading a magazine that was left at the bedside in our hotel room. It included a shocking article about the Thai fishing industry. The story revealed that many Thai fishermen were kidnapped and tortured, finding themselves imprisoned and working for corrupt companies. If the fishermen got sick or tired, he was simply thrown overboard and left to drown. Between this and lifting martial law for the sake of the World Cup being televised, we had a new appreciation for our privilege and safety that awaited us back home. Travelling can also reveal and remind us of where we come from.

The long flight over to Thailand had been painful. Mike's head had exploded, and we'd entered so many time zones I believe we may have slipped in and out of the "upside down" a few times. I had hoped our trip back would be less *Blood Sport* and more *Mary Poppins*, but as it turned out, severe cranial pain would become our travel MO.

We prepared as best we could: assembling peanut butter sammies, downloading playlists, and ensuring our books and pills were in close proximity and could be pulled from the underneath of our seats with ease. You have to be somewhat of a contortionist on flights, especially the ones that are three seats across like those on most international routes. Mike typically sits on the outside seat, so his giraffe legs can stretch out. I typically sit in the middle seat, so the only person I'm bothering every half an hour to pee is my husband. The window seat is a wild card. There have been trips when this seat was left empty and it's better than winning a year's supply of ice cream. Other times it's someone chatty that you might make a Kevin Bacon connection with, OR it might be someone you secretly want to throat punch.

On our flight back from Thailand, the window seat was occupied by a middle-aged Italian guy with a slick moustache, a tight leather jacket, and eyes darker than an empty well. I noticed him before I noticed there were no television screens on the backs of the seats in front of us. It's a gamble nowadays as to whether you'll have the luxury of in-flight entertainment. Most newer planes are equipped with Hollywood blockbusters and re-runs of *Grey's Anatomy*. This trip, in 2014, came with something we're told was meatloaf and a window seat companion that shortly after take-off, slipped into a drug- induced coma.

In hindsight, the sleeping moustache man was the most brilliant traveller I have ever known. He said his name was Tony—a good mobster name, I thought. I told him I'd try not to bother him with my middle-seat-squirming. Those would be the only words we exchanged. As I eagle-armed my way into my backpack in search of something to keep my mind busy for the pending 16-hour flight ahead, Tony—who carried nothing more than his wallet and maybe a moustache comb—popped a handful of pills into his mouth and swallowed them, waterless, as he cozied up against the window. Mike and I exchanged a quick look at each other as we organized our snacks, notebooks, gum, juice, and headphones neatly on the tray tables in front of us. We had exactly one inch of space to exist in for the day.

Tony bent one arm up against the window to rest his moustache face on. It looked a little awkward, kind of like getting stuck in your sweater trying to take it off, but he was fast asleep before the plane left the runway. I wanted those pills.

The first three hours on the flight were absolutely fine. Enjoyable, even. Mike and I chatted about trip highlights, the souvenirs we were coming home with but didn't need, the best pad thai we ate, and the things we hoped to do once we landed in San Francisco. I got up to pee eight times and wrote in my journal. Mike finished reading his book and completed his scan of people-watching in search of characters that might appear in his next novel. By the time hours four and five roll around, your neck and knees start to feel arthritic and anxious. You're now a little irritated at the dainty flight attendants for not having movies available. You'll "never fly this cheap airline again." By hours six to nine you despise everyone who is able to sleep on an airplane, knowing you cannot. I particularly hated Tony who was still fast asleep. Nine hours and this guy hadn't flinched. Isn't he thirsty? Doesn't he have to pee? Doesn't he want to stretch his legs?

Hours nine to 13 are the worst. The air inside the plane starts to feel like a Goodlife sauna filled with people eating Burger King and passing gas. Your body feels like you've run a marathon you didn't train for. Emotions are high, morale is low. All you want is to watch *50 First Dates* and escape the sound of other people's snoring and the mere existence of Tony. You start talking to yourself, reassuring your brain that this won't last forever even though it's already been longer than forever that you've been sitting in your one-inch cube.

I got up to pee again.

Hours 13 to 16, something shifts inside of us. We only have three hours to go. We can do a three-hour flight anytime. Remember, three-hour flights are easy: reminiscing, souvenirs, food, San Francisco, not throat-punching moustache man. Though it felt like I had been holding my breath underwater for a year and my skin was crawling with carbon dioxide and curry, it was almost over.

When the wheels of the flight finally touched American soil, I was overcome with delirium. Exhausted, anxious, achy, hungry, and dirty. Tony's eyes slowly split open and his crooked arm that hadn't moved in almost a day, fell into his lap with ease. He yawned like a drowsy puppy and within seconds was fully alert, hopefully to distribute his magical pills to people like me. Tony was nothing less than a hero to me that day. As prepared and avid of a traveller I believed myself to be, he took the travel gold.

Finally in the terminal of the airport, finally able to walk further than the length of a diving board back and forth, finally able to buy a foot long hotdog, finally able to lay down in a bed, we were overwhelmed with relief.

We had pre-booked a hotel room just two kilometres away from the airport knowing we would be destroyed. Our friend Seabrook would pick us up the next day and we'd stay with him in the Mission district for a week. Though it was in the middle of the day, time zones didn't exist anymore. All we could think about was sleep and solitude. I started tearing my bag apart looking for the name of the hotel so we could hail a cab and collapse onto a pile of polyester bed sheets. I couldn't find anything. I could barely find my own hands at this point, much less the name of a hotel that I had booked six weeks ago in the opposite state of mind that I was in today. I checked my phone for emails, I checked my notebook for scratched-down hotel names, I checked every scrap of paper and receipt in my wallet hoping something would read in thick red marker, "Dear Kristen, I know you're catatonic and currently looking for your hotel room. It's called the Shit-Hole Inn and is at 123 Go the Fuck to Sleep Avenue, California" but that paper never turned up. There I sat, in a sweaty, deflated heap on the cold SFO floors, surrounded by torn paper and tears. I have never been more desperate in my life.

I don't remember what happened next, but believe Mike got on Wi-Fi and figured out where we needed to go. It was during these 20 minutes that my brain and body went into the black hole of hell. Maybe I was inside Tony's eyes. Maybe I was in that well of blackness and pain that could only be masked by fistfuls of sleeping pills and mobster mentality. The next thing I knew we were in a dive motel in the middle of California. While the bright sun shone overhead, my head was buried in a toilet as it throbbed in pain.

It was the first migraine I ever had. Something changed in the neurological makeup of my brain that day. The pain was so intolerable, I could barely speak. I writhed in agony like a beheaded snake. I pleaded with

Mike to go find me Advil. Better yet, get me Tony. Tell him I'll wear the red or blue bandana. I'll be a mule in Mexico, or learn to be the best meth cook in the Midwest. I'd take meetings with bosses or be his maid—just get me the good pills. Poor Mike had no better of a day than I had had. He had endured all of the same thick air, shitty food, and hard airplane seats. He was just as exhausted and hungry as I was, but could see my desperation. I kept vomiting. I kept agonizing and twisting in pain.

The 16-hour flight seemed to leach into the next 24 hours, most of which I spent as the worst version of myself. I ate a chocolate bar and a bottle of Advil and looked as though I was coming off of a heroin addiction. I spent most of the day and night on the cold, cheap tile on the hotel bathroom floor, the migraine hangover almost as intense as the migraine itself. At one point, I floated the idea of staying another night at the shitty hotel. I couldn't move. I couldn't ask my body and my brain to do anything but lay like a landfill of waste in a $69 dollar a night hotel on the outskirts of San Francisco.

With some gentle coaxing and a warm bath, Mike managed to peel me off the floor and into some clean clothes. He checked us out of rehab and we walked next door to an IHOP. We split an order of pancakes that we couldn't finish between the two of us and saw Seabrook's truck roll in to take us onward to our next adventure.

MY FIFTEEN MINUTES

The day before we left for Cuba, I posted a video on my band's Facebook page. Tessa Virtue and Scott Moir had just won the Olympic gold medal for dance pairs figure skating. If someone in Canada at that point said they didn't love Tessa and Scott, they were legally shot in the kneecaps by the RCMP. They were both beautiful, humble, and had a magnetic yet undefined relationship. Were they a couple? Were they secretly in love? It was hard to believe they couldn't be after their provocative numbers on the ice, but no one really knew.

During their gold medal skate, I found myself yelling at the TV like a drunk uncle everyone's embarrassed of. I cursed, I screamed obscenities and encouragement at the screen while their seamless charade of beauty and grace mesmerized the masses. I was amped up and on level 10. While typically portrayed as a dainty and uppity sport for the elite, I couldn't help but bring the passion of a Canadian hockey fan to it.

I got the idea to make a video of a slightly exaggerated version of what I had found myself doing. I set up a tripod and recorded the skate from my computer screen. I traded in the typically quiet and reserved commentary that wouldn't wake a mouse with a more abrasive approach. I thought of local sayings, yelled "JESUS" and "SKATE" a whole lot, and acted like I had smuggled in some rum to a game between the Leafs and Habs in 2003 and Tie Domi was about to throw down.

I posted it online and we drove to the airport hotel. Whenever we have an early flight, we try to stay there. There's free parking and no better way to start of a travel day than with a rock-hard bagel and watery scrambled eggs from a continental breakfast.

It was our annual February 16th anniversary trip.

> **TRAVEL TIP:** *If you're celebrating something, tell EVERYONE you can. We've gotten free chocolate, champagne, and over-the-top smiles (fake but who cares!) just by saying aloud it was our anniversary to people within earshot.*

I put my computer and phone away and tried to live in the moment. This was a milestone. A special time where we got to celebrate who we were as a couple.

We got to our gate at the airport the next day. We'd never been to Cuba and were excited to hopefully pound back some cigars and dark rum. I was fairly knowledgeable about the country because in Grade 10 I had made a video on the Cuban Missile Crisis for a history project. The video, while factual and informative, was so laden with profanity and sexual innuendos that we had to create systematic distractions for the teacher upon our public viewing. In the end the project was so well received, it earned a 15/10 and I didn't have to do the next assignment. My passwords to online banking are still references to those fraught days in 1962, so I'm basically an expert on the country.

As we sat there, a group of people across from us kept looking at me. Then another group. They'd elbow their friends and look in my direction. I'm used to being recognized every once and a while from my band, but this was strange. I figured my best bet was to try to look extra cool. It is, however, a hard thing to pull off while wearing a Clay Aiken T-shirt. Some may even say impossible. I realized it was probably just the stupid shirt everyone was looking at and didn't think much of it as we boarded the plane.

On the way down we lucked out and got to sit in the emergency exit seat. There's a lot of pressure put on you when you're in this aisle. I don't really want that responsibility but I definitely want more leg room so I take the challenge. The flight attendants come over and are always so serious. "Are you prepared in case of an emergency?" they ask, looking directly into the depths of your soul. I never want to be a downer, so I always give a thumbs up and "All good here" type remark. The reality is that if we're lucky enough to survive the free fall at 600 miles per hour from 30,000 feet, I don't think it's going to matter too much if I followed the 48-second rundown of emergency prep guidelines. A mad panic will ensue. Whether I sat in the exit seat or not, I'll be crawling over mutilated corpses and elbowing crying babies in a hysterical rage to fight for my survival. Limbs will be spread haphazardly through the cabin, screams of agony will fill the air, and blood ... there will be SO much blood. I've seen the movie *Alive*. It didn't matter who was in the emergency exit row. They had to eat ass meat.

The lady came over and asked us to memorize something in Spanish that we had to say in case the plane went down. I just nodded, gave a thumbs up and repeatedly said, "Si!" over and over. I can only assume that the sentence represented something along the lines of: "THE PLANE HAS CRASHED AND IF YOU'RE SOMEHOW STILL ALIVE FIGHT FOR YOUR LIFE IN ANY WAY POSSIBLE!" Besides, if we did go down and in the bloody madness that ensued someone turned to me and asked "Were you seated in the emergency exit row? What's the plan here?" I would take whatever energy I have in my bleeding body to punch them (or kick them depending on what limbs I have left) firmly in the nose.

We got to our resort, threw our luggage in the room, and got ready for the beach. I put on the classic "Canadian on vacation" outfit: tank top I'm too embarrassed to wear around people who know me, ugly multicolour surf shorts that depict some bizarre tropical scene involving pelicans and hula dancers, cheap flip-flops, and a ball cap. We held hands and made our way towards the white sand. We thought we should probably write our parents to let them know we weren't captured and forced into a labour camp picking bananas for the commies.

Internet in Cuba is basically the equivalent to small-town dial-up in 1998. We stopped in the lobby and tried to get online. I waited for Facebook to open and ordered a piña colada. The bartender was a Russian guy name Sergei. "Like the hockey player," he started. "Fedorov," I finished. He high-fived me and we were best friends for the week.

I looked down at my phone. The number of notifications from Facebook read 26,542. "What the hell?!" I said under my breath. Kristen came over. New notifications were coming in every second. It was a blitzkrieg of Facebook action, an all-out bombardment of alerts and pop-ups.

I clicked on the red bell indicating the surplus of notifications. The video I posted the day prior had almost a million views. It was shared tens of thousands of times and had new comments coming in every second. It had effectively gone viral.

I opened my email. News outlets from around the country wanted to talk to me, and our band's social media numbers had doubled.

"What. The. Fuck!?" I said aloud. Kristen laughed. Sergei looked at me. "You okay, Big Guy?" he asked.

"I'm great, actually," I told him.

I wasn't sure what to do. It was mesmerizing seeing something literally go viral in front of my eyes. Every second there was a new alert. It was spreading like wildfire and completely out of my hands. I decided that the gods of the internet were in charge and there was nothing I could do. I turned the phone off and said we need to get to the beach.

We spent the day in the sun, swimming, playing ping-pong, drinking piña coladas, and laughing our asses off.

That evening when we went out for dinner, I looked at my phone again. The video was still gaining momentum and had over a million views. I just smiled and shook my head.

The next morning when I opened my phone back up, the video was gone. There was a notification from the International Olympic Committee that said we had illegally used their copyrighted material. Any further posts would result in the loss of our social media channels. And that was that.

We celebrated our second anniversary and did all the things you do at an all-inclusive resort: eat and drink your face off, get so sunburned you can't move for half the week you're there, etc. It's normally not our preferred way to see places, but sometimes it sure is easy.

When we got back to Halifax, I tried contacting the IOC to get the video reinstated. I never got any further than talking to a robot who told me where the next Olympics were being hosted. It didn't matter though. Our band's audience had grown significantly. We had new fans that we could try to promote our music to. For months after I couldn't go anywhere without people stopping me on the street to say they saw the video.

I put every ounce of who I am into the songs I put out. I put countless hours into my recordings, into trying to grow as a musician, songwriter and entertainer. At that point in time, the thing that my band was most known for was a ridiculous video of me doing commentary over a figure-skating routine. I guess it's better than not being known at all.

DRAGULA:

Love Story #9

Drag queens in San Francisco are like cowboys in Texas; they're plentiful, highly skilled and have multiple pairs of fantastic shoes. My hometown had a population of 83 humans and 500 cows. Of those 83 humans, none of them were drag queens. Mike grew up in an old coal mining town where at least half the people were on pogey (employment insurance) and the other half wore pogey boots (those big green rubber ones). There weren't any drag queens there either.

In San Francisco, drag queens were everywhere: hitchhiking, Walgreens, checking out *Macbeth* at the library. They were like sculptures you'd see in a museum but with better hair and ability to entertain.

We were staying with our friends, Seabrook and Bonnie. We likely weren't the best house guests after our long flight, but we were grateful for a place to recuperate. In San Fran, we learned that recuperation meant party at a wild drag show.

Dragula was more than a dozen, towering, vivacious queens waving umbrellas and spraying strangers with oversized shlong squirt-guns. It was feathers and bloody fangs meets cock-tales and fire swallowing. Drinks were glowing, served by spike-collared men with breasts bigger than stew pots. I looked over at Mike. My Atlantic Canadian, plaid-shirt wearing, hamburger-eating sports-fan husband and wondered how he was holding up. It's important to check in on each other while travelling. You can't expect your companions to always be in the same head space or mood. Especially given near-death migraines and IHOP pancakes were only just in our recent past. Much to my delight, Mike was partying hard between Heidi Haux and Misty Meaner. Cheering for the ventriloquist on stage and clinking glasses with the snake charmer on the dance floor, I was reminded that he would never drag me down.

MY FEET:

Injuries and Stuff

I'm not sure why, but something always happens to my feet while travelling. They're magnets for sharp, stabby things that you don't want your feet to be magnets for. I once caught a fish and, realizing I didn't have any means to cook it—or if it was actually edible— kicked it off the dock and back into the water. The spikes I didn't know it had, sliced a perfectly linear pattern of holes in me. In Thailand I stepped on old coral that sliced me up like butter. That, plus the kabillion fly bites. My feet are cheesecake to weird bugs. They snack on my sockless feet at all hours of the day; most of the time I can't even tell until there's a dripping, itchy hole adding to the numbers. I tried to count them a few days into our trip and lost track at 70. On one foot. We later came across a place where you could dip your feet into a fish tank with thousands of tiny *Garra rufa* fish that eat away your dead skin. It's an ancient therapeutic method and supposedly really good for you. When I stepped in line to do it, the guy looked at my feet and gave a horrified expression akin to seeing your grandparents have sex. He disappeared for a bit and came back with a roll of tape. He wrapped that tape around my feet for what seemed like hours. In the end he covered up about 93 per cent of my battered paws. The fish had a good time with the remaining seven per cent.

In Costa Rica, I popped a chain on a bike going uphill and the spokes stabbed me in my Achilles tendon. It looked like I was bitten by a shark. And that's what I told people, too. "You ever see the movie *Jaws*?" I'd say, "Coulda been a lot worse!" Again, that plus the hundreds of bleeding, pus dripping fly bites made me look like my feet went through a blender. This might be the reason my feet swelled up like a balloon. I was either allergic to one of the weird bugs, or being kind of chubby and walking 20 kilometres in the heat could have done it too. Luckily, pretty much everyone I met on that trip was a nurse or doctor. Maybe the universe knew these were the people I needed. Thirty seconds into conversations I'd be shoving my bloody feet to the face of strangers and asking, "This look infected or wha?"

In Jamaica on the day after our wedding, I stepped on a sea urchin. The best way to describe a sea urchin for someone who's never seen one is that it's basically a ball of fucking spikes. I was swimming with Kristen, one of our first real moments together as a married couple. I felt a sharp pain in my foot when I put it down. "Something bit me!" I yelled. Before I even finished the sentence, Kristen rocketed towards the shore faster than any Olympic swimmer has ever tread through water. I'd never seen her move so quick. Especially since she's terrified in the water and I didn't know she could actually swim. Thanks, new wife!

I swam to the shore with a throbbing pain in my foot. When I reached the beach, I realized that I'd been punctured with about 50 sharp needle-like objects. Blood dripped from my foot and Kristen ran to the lifeguard. I started to pick the needles out as the drug dealer/lifeguard/photographer approached.

"You step on sea urchin, mon!" he told me.

"Sea urchin? That sounds bad!"

"No, mon . . . as long as you get the needles out the poison won't hurt you."

"Did you just say poison?" I asked. He couldn't have. My luck wasn't *that* bad. I knew that things were supposed to happen to my feet—that's just my MO. But poison? That wasn't part of the deal.

"Yeah, mon, sea urchins are poisonous," he said nonchalantly.

I sped up my needle removal.

I started to feel dizzy. The poison must have been sinking in. I'd be married for one day and then kick the bucket. My accomplishments as a married man were tying my wife in a ping pong match and drinking six Krazy Koconuts without having to take a leak.

"What do I do?" I asked

"Mon," he began, "all you have to do is pee on your foot!"

"You want me to piss on my foot?"

"Yeah mon!"

"What about the poison?"

"You're in beautiful Jamaica; don't worry about the poison!"

People from Nova Scotia don't typically deal with a lot of poisonous creatures in the wild. Sometimes a beaver will cut down a tree you're using for a clothesline, or a racoon will radically alter your world by knocking over a compost bin. He might as well have said I'd been bit by the deadliest snake in the universe, that my internal organs were shutting down as we spoke.

He gave a peace sign and walked away.

I pulled out the last few needles as Kristen frantically tried to help. I knew it was no use. The poison would soon be through my body and I'd take my last breaths on the beach as Bob Marley songs played in the distance guiding me towards the light.

I saw the drink guy going by and asked for another Krazy Koconut. Dying without a delicious, regionally made sugary drink in my hand was never the way I wanted to go.

I limped back to our room sipping on the cocktail and hugging my new wife.

I told her I loved her and that I was trying my hardest at ping-pong earlier that day. I didn't want her to have any doubts on her mind as I crossed over.

When we got to our room I jumped in the shower and pissed with all my strength onto my foot. I let the medicine sink in for a few minutes before washing it off and laying on the bed to think of my last words. I thought of maybe singing one of my own songs; that would be kind of a romantic way to go out. There was the option to quote something meaningful to me, something that changed my perspective on life. I thought of all the things that influenced me along the way: the people, the places, the art that fundamentally transformed my being.

"You break my record . . . now I break you, like I break your friend," I said aloud, calling upon the movie I had watched most in my life, the 1988

Jean Claude Van Damme masterpiece *Bloodsport*.

"What are you talking about?" Kristen inquired as I faded away.

"Very good . . . but brick not hit back . . . ."

I closed my eyes. This was it. The poison would take me to the other side to be united with my predeceased ancestors.

Time passed.

I slowly opened my eyes, expecting the white lights, a welcoming crowd of dead pets and relatives who've watched over my every second the past 30-odd years; there for me every step of the way as I grew, learned, and masturbated, too.

But nothing. I was there in my comfy bed in Jamaica, half-drunk from the sugary booze but still kicking.

I wasn't dead. And I wasn't going to die. That wasn't how it was scripted for me. There were too many journeys left ahead for us, so many undiscovered places and paths to go down. This was just the start of it. Maybe I'd step on poisonous creatures here and there, but we'd get through it. We had each other and that was all that mattered. That and the piss on my foot that saved my life.

ESCOBAR'S ESTATE AND THE WORSHIP ROCK

The Rock of Guatape, better known locally as La Penol, is a popular landmark located on the outskirts of two small towns: Guatape and El Penol, both of which lay claim to ownership of the well-known tourist attraction. The rock's spectacular size and shape make it a mythical attraction, rich with speculation. Its silhouette reminded me of an overturned thimble, fit for the thumb of a giant. Legend argues the birth of the almost 700-foot mountainous stone is nothing more than geology at work, where others believe it is an ancient god to be worshipped and adored. Either way, not only can you go see this marvellous mountain, you can climb it.

With only one remaining day in Medellin, we wanted to travel outside the city for a glimpse of rural Colombia. A two-hour day trip to the Rock of Guatape seemed like the perfect destination. Our hotel concierge booked Mike and me on a bus tour that outlined the itinerary of visiting and climbing the enormous rock and back to the hotel by dinner time.

We boarded the bus and scanned the other passengers with curiosity. We chose a seat behind another couple who quickly struck up conversation. Alfredo, originally from Peru, and his wife Christine from New York. A foreign diplomat at the United Nations and yoga instructor, respectively. As we waited for last minute tourists to make their way to the bus, I could feel I had to pee. This is always the most stressful part of travelling for me. My bladder's the size of a walnut and I usually pee every 30 minutes. I wish this was an exaggeration. Having to hold in my pee is something I've come to accept but if given the opportunity for a more comfortable experience, I'm going to take it. The only time this was really an issue was the time I was solo travelling in Costa Rica and asked the bus driver to pull over so I could whizz on the side of the road. He obliged, and the moment my pants were down around my ankles, started to drive away. I took off running, spilling items from my purse and dribbling on my legs as I caught up with my only means of safety and transportation. A bus full of locals, laughing themselves sick, took great pleasure in the gringa's inability to hold it until the end of the line. I was mortified and terrified all at once as I imagined what it would have been like had they left me behind.

I was off to a better start already having Mike and two new friends to accompany me on this ride. However, I did have to pee and two hours seemed like an awfully long time to hold it. I told myself that maybe South Americans had better manners and would give me five minutes to run to the public washroom I could see in the distance. When I asked the driver, he agreed to stay put and I dashed over to the stainless-steel stall. When I was finished, I opened the stall door and to my despair saw the bus driving away. What is it with this practical joke?! Why was Mike letting them leave?! I started running at lightning speed, anxiety and sadness washing over me. How did I find myself in this bathroom chaos in Latin America all over again?! The bus came to a rolling stop and I flailed myself aboard. Mike explained they were simply pulling up closer to me so I wouldn't have to run as far back to them.

Though unscheduled, we stopped at a quaint roadside snack house that served fried bread for $1. I don't know how much cash we brought with us that day, but we spent it all on *arepas*—some for us, some for the stray dogs that circled our legs.

Our second unscheduled stop was much longer and elaborate than the arepas stand. The tour advertised a roundtrip to the Rock of Guatape and we had just landed in a second mystery town in less than an hour. This time, we were told we were boarding a boat and would be sailing to one of Pablo Escobar's estates. I recalled two things: our hotel claimed not to book with ANY tour company that offered tourist dollars to "his" attractions and, secondly, no one in our group had signed up for *any* of the places we had been so far. In the middle of nowhere Colombia, in the company of a tour guide, a bus driver, and a handful of other tourists who spoke neither Spanish nor English, we boarded the boat destined for Escobar's second-biggest estate.

The boat ride through the widening river was decadent. The Colombian landscape sagged with glowing green branches and mattress thick moss. The hills looked computer generated with perfectly placed blades of grass and time released exotic birds whiter than the cocaine that surely spattered the coastline. Mike and I were at the squared off stern of the boat, the soft rumbling engine propelling us through the blue waters as tree branches wisped over the surface. We rounded a bend and to the right sat a sprawling collection of buildings and abandoned structures. It was Escobar's house.

I didn't want to be, but I was very excited as we stepped onto the private island and given all access passes to the remains of the estate. We were told, despite its enormous size, that Escobar visited this place fewer than five times. Once was for his daughter's birthday where he hired a veterinarian to sew real swan wings and a rhino horn onto a horse so it would look like a unicorn. The horse died the next day.

Among the remains we saw Escobar's swimming pool, sauna room, guest houses, and games rooms. Almost all of the buildings were peppered with bullet holes or worse. You couldn't help but feel a part of the power that embodied the brick walls of the building, dilapidated or not. We grew arrogant under the sheer presence of the drug lord's history and, for a moment, felt the appeal of belonging to the power held by the Medellin cartel.

We assumed our next stop had to be the rock. The bus was approaching the entrance to the giant structure, but much to our surprise, we only caught a glimpse before veering off onto another road. Apparently, we were on route to our third unscheduled stop. As much as I appreciated getting more than we had bargained for, I also worried our real final destination would never be seen.

Landing in Guatape town was like being plopped inside a crayon box. It was Charlie and the Chocolate Factory meets Picasso; painted buildings, smells of ice cream and coffee circulating the streets, shops with handy crafts, and to my great amusement, several art galleries. We had 45 minutes to spend in the town (though any length of time would have been acceptable given we had no idea we would be coming here in the first place). We spent approximately 43 minutes of our allotted time visiting artists in their galleries, hearing stories, and collecting artwork—the only kind of souvenirs we ever buy.

By this time, my heart was full and while I still believed we had booked the wrong tour, was willing to accept the special day for what it was. I half fell asleep on Mike's shoulder as the bus began the journey back to Medellin. We were both exhausted from a full day of activities and settled into conversation with Christine and Alfredo for the return trip.

This of course, was the moment we FINALLY pulled into the entrance of the giant rock.

There are 649 stairs that run zigzag along the face of the rock. You pay money to climb them, which on your best day is daunting. In the fatigued state we were in, it felt next to impossible, but the temptation of adventure took over. Bending your neck back as far it goes allows you to take in the full picture of the grand presence of the rock. The climb was both intimidating and otherworldly. The view from step 100 is breathtaking. The view from the top was truly surreal. A 360-degree landscape of nothing but islands, water, mist, and magic. We stayed at the top for a long time. We looked around in silence, knowing we were somewhere special. Of all the places we had sought a spectacular view, this place was incomparably the greatest of them all. It was a sweet, serene, sensory journey. Christine and Alfredo emerged behind us from step 649 and we saw in their faces how we were feeling. While geology may have offered this shape, the Rock of Guatape was unquestionably a God worthy of our worship.

"VENEZUELA"

We sat on the waterfront in Cartagena and ate one of the most delicious burritos we've ever had. We'd been travelling for about three weeks by this point, into the thick of it all and were starting to feel in unison with our surroundings. Our bellies were full and we watched the sun set over the historic city. We were 4,000 kilometers from home, surrounded by good food, drinks, natural beauty, and that feeling you get when you travel, the reason you do it in the first place.

A man and a woman with two small boys approached us. The kids were around six and seven. They held onto their parents' hands and didn't make a sound. Their eyes were big and sad, something the eyes of a child should never be.

As the burrito and beer poured down our throats, the man started to speak to us in Spanish. Instantly, without thinking, we didn't want anything to do with them. Cartagena is a city of sales. It's a constant barrage of bargaining and overly aggressive people trying to sell you things. That's how people make their living. Everyone has something they think your life will be made better by having, and is there to offer you the deal of a lifetime. And in a city like that, where you're constantly bombarded with sales pitches and pushy people 24/7, your initial reaction is a simple "no thanks." You don't even pay attention to them. You've already passed by 500 people that day that you didn't pay attention to. There's no reason to start now.

As soon as they approached, I instinctively said the same thing I did to all the others that day, to water salesmen, giant aphrodisiac ant salesmen, the women impressively balancing fruits on their heads, drug dealers, hat salesmen, and every other person trying to make a buck: "No gracias!" That's when they typically switch over to broken English and say something like "Oh Big Guy . . . you need this ants for your wee wee . . . wife will like it! Make you very, very big penis!" I'll then seamlessly switch over to my native tongue and give a definitive, "No thanks, bud!"

This man did not switch over to limited English, which was strange for a Colombian schemer. Every person who sells something in a foreign country can at least say: "Good deal _____ on!" or "My friend! This _____ what you need!"

I told them that I couldn't speak Spanish. And I can't. I can order my go to chicken with garlic meal off a menu, thank someone, and ask for up to six beers at a time (the intro of "Pretty Fly for a White Guy" by the Offspring only counted to six, so in the scenario where seven of anything is needed, I'm out).

I told the man "No Español," and determined that the phone cases, trinkets, and condoms he may have been offering were of no use to me.

He started to repeat the word "Venezuela" over and over. At the time, Venezuela was not in a good place. I didn't exactly know why, but a mass exodus of their people was happening. I try to pay attention to what's going on in the world, but it's hard to be deeply familiar with the political situations of all 195 countries. Things to me are typically either good or bad. I knew that at that moment, things were bad in Venezuela. The details to anything like this are usually a long, lengthy narrative of corruption, rebellion, and conflict. The intricacies for someone on the outside can be tough to really put together properly.

He talked in Spanish with a passion that, to me, just meant he was likely a really, really good sunglasses salesmen. I just shrugged my shoulders and said, "No Español!" again. He kept repeating "Venezuela," his body language becoming more and more deflated.

When he realized that the one word that we both understood was not going to help, he walked a few steps away from us with his family to talk amongst themselves. I clearly can't speak Spanish, but Kristen can.

She listened in. The man turned to his wife and told her we don't understand them, that we won't help. The mom turned to the little kids, her eyes watery. "It's going to be alright," she said. "Momma will find us food." She squeezed the little boys by the shoulders and looked them in the eyes. "Momma will do whatever she has to!"

There was a look in her eyes. Something I'd never really seen in real life before. It was utter desperation, it was fear, and it was bravery.

Kristen realized what was happening and told me what was going on.

This was not someone trying to sell us something. This was a family that had fled a country in turmoil. They had hit a breaking point. They needed food, somewhere to stay. It wasn't a scam and they weren't looking for money for drugs. They were trying to survive.

When we saw the tears in the father's eyes and the mom reassuring her two little boys that everything would be alright, we realized it was different. They were people down on their luck. A few things went the wrong way and all of a sudden, you're homeless in another country with no money.

When you see people like that you start to understand crime. You understand how someone could turn to robbery, to becoming a drug mule. All the parents cared about was their own family. They didn't want to be begging for money. I could tell how hard it was for them to do it. But they did because they'd do anything for each other. Like anyone, anywhere in the world would.

I'll never forget the look on the mom's face. She would have fought an army, climbed a mountain barefoot, or cut off her arms just so her kids could be alright. And there's nothing more powerful than that—when someone gets to the point where they're willing to do anything, they're willing to die.

They were a young couple, probably our age. They were dressed normal, both attractive, and the kids were well-behaved. They could have been us. They were just a family who fled a bad place to try and make a better life. We, on the other hand, had flown across the world to be there by choice, eating at four different restaurants a day, seeking out gelato spots, googling "Best Dessert in Cartagena." We may not be millionaires, but compared to them we were Bill and Melinda Gates. We went there to experience a different culture. They were there because everything they knew and loved in their home went to hell.

We had to do something.

As they started to walk away, I yelled out to them. "Señor, señor!" He turned around. I don't know how much we had on us but we emptied our pockets out and gave them all the pesos we had. It wasn't a lot. It might have been $50 or $60 at the most. The man started to cry. Tears streamed down his face and he got down on his knees. He put his hands together in prayer formation and looked up to the sky like he was thanking God. The mother was shaking she was so happy, the sad eyes on the kids turned into inquisitive, hopeful eyes that every child deserves to have.

In a few days we'd fly home. We'd go to the house we own, turn on the lights, drink water from our tap, and fill our fridge with groceries we buy around the corner from us. I'd have my struggles: getting shows, trying to get more social media followers, and trying to write songs people can relate to. Kristen would have to deal with a messy studio, expensive materials, and figuring out ways to market abstract art to stay relevant. It's not the easiest life in the world, but it's far from hard.

They walked away holding hands. We finished our meal and left in silence. The sun set and the streets came alive with the energy and spirit of a Latin American city at night.

We got back to Canada a few days later. I thought of the family. I thought of the little boys. I hoped that wherever they were their stomachs were full and they were laughing, kicking a soccer ball around with other kids their age, Mom and Dad laughing and drinking piña coladas as they watched on. I hoped they found a place to stay, maybe overlooking the ocean and a good school nearby. Dad got a good job as a security guard at one of the museums and Mom was working at a daycare. I smiled to myself thinking about it, but knew deep down, it probably wasn't true.

New Orleans to New York City:

Accidental Layover

A week in New Orleans feels like a combination of being at a carnival high on psychedelics and working as an extra in a David Lynch film. Our first hour in the boisterous city had us brushing shoulders with Bernie Sanders in the most luxurious Pride parade ever marched, laden with beads and rainbow flavoured condoms, thrown from the hennaed hands of marching unicorns.

We had heard of a dive bar that Brad and Angelina used to frequent. It was called The Abbey and served a bottle of Pabst Blue Ribbon with a shot of Fireball whisky for five bucks. This seemed like a good deal *and* activity for 2 p.m. on our second day in NOLA. It was either day drunk or alligator hunting, and $10 into my day, I knew I had made the right decision. The dimly lit bar was outfitted with old bottles and tokens of drowned sorrows past, just the right touches to complement our musings that were growing louder by the minute. By 4 p.m. Mike led me and my lack of composure onto the streets to dance with the jazz bands. They seemed to be everywhere and tipped their hats in a way that made me blush.

By sundown, we escorted our healthy buzz from piano bars to blues clubs. Between the music, witchery, history, and freedom to express, NOLA was a blast. After a week of rainbow patterned thongs, street music, and the best fried chicken known to humankind, we packed up our jazz hands and headed to the airport.

You always run the risk of ending a vibrant trip with a dreary airport encounter. Our flight route home included a layover in New York. When we landed there in the early evening, we were informed of a 24-hour delay. Maybe it was the remnants of the grits and glitter, or maybe it was our infatuation with NYC, but this was music to our ears. We asked if we could extend the 24 hours into 72 hours and get on a flight back to Halifax a few days later. The indifferent and somewhat perplexed receptionist obliged, printed us food vouchers for our "troubles" and sent us off to a five-star hotel on Long Beach for the night.

The hotel was made of onyx and diamonds with an endless view of beautiful beach runners, exercising their genetically modified pets. We toasted room service champagne in robes thicker than the winter jackets we'd soon be wearing at home, and relished in the ability to make ice cream out of ice.

We wandered around Central Park on the anniversary of September 11th. It was unseasonably warm, the sun as bright and beautiful as it's ever been. We weren't supposed to be in New York, but there was no other place in the world we'd rather be. We laid in a grassy field, the greatest city in the world all around us, the buildings visible off in the distance as they peeked over the towering treeline. We looked up at the sky, our backs on the green grass, our hands and hearts locked and smiles impossibly large. The city buzzed all around us but we just lay there—the person we care for most in the world at our side, soaking in the beauty of an unplanned moment, the best moment.

THINGS WE SAW THAT SHOULD BE EVERYWHERE

One of the reasons we travel is to be exposed to new ideas. Immersing yourself in different cultures opens your eyes to new ways that life can be lived. You realize that what you do, and the way the place you live in functions, isn't necessarily the best. Here are a number of observations based on what we've learned elsewhere which would make life in North America exponentially better.

The Chicken Glove

The first meal we got in Medellin was fried chicken. When Kristen sees any type of establishment selling fried chicken, she immediately transforms into the equivalent of a heroin addict who needs her fix. I told her I'd treat her and order. That's basically comparable to buying any other girl a diamond ring and a yacht so I figured I'd do my job and be a good husband.

They didn't speak English at this place, so I pointed at the picture of fried chicken on the menu. The man at the counter gave me the world's most complicated receipt that had hundreds of checkmarks and numbers on it. I don't think a mathematician at MIT could have figured it out, so I just tapped my Visa and gave him a thumbs up. He gave a thumbs up back and passed me two plastic gloves and a plate of fried chicken. I had no idea what the glove was for, but brought it back to my smiling and excited wife along with the greasy, heart attack on a plate. Beside us, a man put on his plastic glove and began to eat with that hand. It was a chicken glove.

We followed suit and each slid on our own gloves. It was glorious. You could eat a zoo's worth of fried chicken and not even have to wipe your hand at the end. I wanted to move there instantly. Why couldn't every meal be like this? Why couldn't every restaurant just hand out a plastic glove and let you go to town? We ate with our plastic glove on one hand and held hands with our other. If any of these ideas should be adopted, the chicken glove is number one.

Drinking in Public

A number of places in the world allow public consumption of alcohol.

Drinking. On the street.

Drinking. Anywhere you want to.

This is the greatest thing in the world (after the chicken glove, of course). In Canada, to drink in public you have to pour rum into a plastic bottle and act like you're 14 and Mom may come around the corner to check on you and your friends at any second. To have a beer in a park, you have to cut open an empty can of pop, remove the top and bottom with surgical precision and create a perfect aluminium deception device to wrap seamlessly around your can to stave off a $500 fine. In Europe, you just do whatever the hell you want. You can walk into any store, ANYWHERE, buy a can of beer, a bottle of gin, or mix a goddamn strawberry daiquiri and just start drinking. They even have bottle openers at the cash register and open them for you if you want to start drinking before you exit the store. If you can't wait the two seconds it takes to walk outside, they will allow you to—actually encourage you to—begin drinking inside their premises.

Parking Anywhere

One of the best things about developing countries is that you can park wherever the hell you want. There are no parking meters, no laws on which way you're supposed to be facing, or any indication that you shouldn't just randomly leave your car on a sidewalk. It's a free-for-all that seems to magically work perfectly. You don't have to keep change in your pocket or figure out some futuristic parking meter that you need a degree from Stanford to use.

Pad Thai and Coconut Smoothies

If I was blindfolded anywhere in Thailand, at any time of day or night, in 30 seconds with ease I could still find an old, friendly woman with missing teeth and a weathered face who makes the best pad thai and coconut smoothies you've ever tasted.

It's so inexpensive you feel bad. I used to mow lawns as a summer job when I was a kid. I got paid $20 for an average lawn. It would usually take a little more than an hour and it wasn't very hard. If I took the money I was paid for even just one lawn that summer, I could eat like a king in Thailand.

If our government truly wants to make our country the best it can be, they would grant citizenship to as many of these amazing women who wanted it, pay them the salary of an NHL player, and let them work their magic. Life would be exponentially better.

For me, a perfect evening would be to drive downtown and park without needing to scrounge for loose change, eat a greasy piece of chicken without having to wipe my hands, get shitfaced in a public park without having to worry about going to the slammer, and finish the night off by ordering a pad thai and smoothie to ward of tomorrow's hangover.

My dreams are big, but I believe in them. Someday, I know this utopia can exist. In the meantime, I'll get through my days knowing that the future is bright; that a necessary change is coming.

STRESSED IN SAVASANA

I've been practising yoga for almost 15 years. It feels funny to talk about that kind of time frame, but here I am, somewhere between 30 and 40 making jokes and references to old age in the ways I always heard adults exchange but didn't really understand. I understand now. Mike asked me the other day how long it had been since I had last gone roller-blading.

"Probably 10 years ago?" I thought.

"You went roller blading when you were 28?!" he asked with equal parts amazement and disbelief. I did the math and realized I was probably more like 13. That's 25 gross years ago and it felt like such an unnatural timeline that my brain immediately resorted to a more tolerable "decade ago" response. It's both bothersome and beautiful to reflect on all those years ago. It's also one of the reasons I keep up with my yoga practice on a regular basis. Flexibility, breath, strength, all components to health and youthfulness. When you're travelling in a place like LA, you're reminded regularly of the contrast between rock-hard-muscle-beach-abs and not-quite-set-Jell-O-Nova Scotia-abs. A week into vacation (more specifically, vacation food) I thought I better take my Jell-O belly to the yoga studio.

I am a long-time member of the Modo Hot Yoga Studio in Halifax. I like the heat, and despite trying many other styles and studios, this is the space I feel most at ease. The staff know me by name and have lent me leggings and water bottles when I forgot to bring my own. I am familiar with most of the instructors and their teaching style. I know the days and times of my favourite classes. I know what locker I prefer to use and recognize many other members of the studio. Modo Halifax even sells my custom-designed yoga leggings and has invited me to host art shows in their space.

I had attended yoga classes many times before while travelling: Costa Rica, Thailand, Jamaica, Cuba, but going to a class in Venice, Los Angeles, felt different. I felt nervous.

One of the lovely parts of yoga is that there is no "wrong way" of practising, at least this was the instruction I received from the teachers I liked best. One teacher at Modo once said at the beginning of her class, "If you want to just come and lay on your mat and breathe for 90 minutes, you're doing yoga." I felt *amazing* at yoga in that moment. And really grateful that someone finally validated that napping was indeed exercise.

I didn't hear or expect that same piece of advice in Venice. I sensed the air thicken with pretentiousness as I neared the studio, just a two-mile walk away from our hotel on Venice Beach. The women at the reception desk were preoccupied with a gift bag overflowing with expensive gifts that a "client" had left behind. They took turns pulling carefully wrapped items out of the bag, admiring their worth and desirability. It seemed most of the items were made from kale or alkaline water. I didn't know what alkaline water was but there sure was a lot of it in LA. One of the women finally spoke, acknowledging a human was standing in front of her. Without making eye contact, she turned an iPad around on a swivel bar and instructed me to fill out a waiver. After an awkward 10 minutes of semi-conversing with the clichéd receptionist distracted by the calorie count on her kale bar, I was escorted to the change room. I pulled my backpack, filled with second-hand workout clothes, closer to my body. I waved goodbye to Mike who had walked me down. He was grabbing a beer at a pub while I attended class. How I had wished the tables were turned.

I was given instructions on how to use the locker room. Apparently, it can be more complicated than changing your clothes. In Halifax, I had never once used a lock on my locker and had usually exchanged smiles and several "How are yous?" by now. I found myself taking trial runs, practising how the new-age space ship lockers in Venice worked before I actually stored my contents inside. "That was really smart of you," I thought to myself, as I mastered the hardware on the lock. I took my faded Puma shorts, sports bra I've had since high school, and borrowed hotel towel into the studio.

There were five guys in the studio already, each of whom resembled a cross between Bruce Lee and Conor McGregor. Tattoos, muscles, sweat, and very expensive yoga attire. Not Lululemon expensive, but brands whose names were printed in metallic gold, accented with hand-stitched seams and built-in acupuncture technology. I put my mat at the back of the room. And then moved it. And then moved it again. I then became self-conscious because I had moved my mat three times and was certainly drawing attention to myself. Girls with matching lavender-coloured suits started to filter into the hot space, their water bottles more beautiful and expensive than my plane ticket to land myself there in the first place. My water bottle was from the Dollar Store.

The studio felt more like a concert hall than an intimate practice space. The high ceilings rivalled those at the Bellagio and echoed like screams in the Grand Canyon. Being deaf in one ear, I found the acoustics disorientating. When the instructor started class, I had to keep craning my neck up to see what was going on. Not because I didn't understand the poses, but because I couldn't hear what they were.

The postures were no more difficult than other classes I had attended. We held our planks a little longer and there was a pointed obsession with our toes being "pigeoned in" and knees bent "especially for those who know they can be straightened," but I managed to keep up well enough that my skills didn't stand out as much as my cheap shorts. There were gleaming, rock-hard bodies surrounding me, many of which I'm sure were sculpted under the capable knives on Rodeo Drive. Perfectly manicured gel nails gripped yoga mats that likely doubled as magic carpets. I spent most of the class time daydreaming about the doughnuts Mike promised we would have afterwards.

We finished the class in the amount of time it would take to carve a toothpick from a sequoia and I watched half a dozen people organize their blocks and straps before I rose from *savasana*. I needed to see where the MMA fighters and runway models put their shit so I could follow suit. Pretending I was in deep relaxation, I laid with one eye open, monitoring what my next steps were supposed to be. Soon after, I scrambled out of the Taj Mahal room and felt relief wash over me.

I opened my locker with ease, for I had used my four-digit banking code to encrypt the space ship lock. I was basically Neil Armstrong. In the shower, one of my earrings fell out and rolled into the stall next to me. All I could see was a pair of feet, just inches from the tack-like stem of my upside down earring. I snatched it quickly and stayed a little longer under the hot water, likely alkaline, so the mystery feet and her judgment could leave first. I walked back to my locker, having to ask a woman to please shuffle aside as she was blocking the entire back corner's worth of space. She hated me for asking. I turned the dial around in circles, spelling out my banking password. I was on the home stretch! Mike would be outside, ready to take me for fried bread covered in icing and sprinkles.

And then nothing. The door wouldn't budge. Why wasn't it opening?! I was sweating more now than I had in the 102-degree class. I assumed the locker code would remain the same but must have reset when I went into the shower. FUUUUCK. There were two women left in the locker room. One was the lady who now hated me for politely asking her to allow me to my locker, the other was mystery feet and may very well hate me too.

"Excuse me," I said shyly to the locker-blocker woman, "would you mind asking the front desk for a locker key, please?" The two women who hated me looked at each other sideways, a silent coin toss about who would complete the disgusting favour requested by the Canadian stray. "It's just, I don't want to walk out into the reception area in my towel," I had to explain, as though it was a mystery. I thought about home. I thought about how a whole room full of women would have offered to get the key for me. They'd call a locksmith from their cellphone if they had to. I was mortified, but also felt for the first time in the past two hours like the "better" person. I realized how much better it was to be kind and com-passionate than mean and plastic. I thought about how yoga was about inner peace and joy, not biceps and bragging rights. I was proud of my faded sports bra that had seen thousands of hours of practice, my no-name water bottle that had travelled across the world and, most importantly, my courage for trying something new and being the black sheep amongst the well-groomed show ponies.

I ate two doughnuts with Mike that evening as we held hands under the stars on the Venice Beach pier.

THINKING IN LA

Day 1

I was sick as a dog when leaving and afraid my head might explode like it did in Thailand. I ordered a hot toddy in the Halifax airport restaurant from a middle-aged woman. She said I reminded her of her son and took care of me like a mom would. It was snowing pretty bad and our flight was delayed. We knew we'd miss our connection in Newark but negotiated a free hotel there so flew anyway. Our shuttle driver on the way to the Robert Treat Hotel was amazing. His name was Terry and he had more charisma than Barack Obama and Mr. T rolled into one glorious human. He gave us the history of the hotel we were staying at. Four American presidents had stayed there. Someone possibly murdered. That or electricity invented there. I can't quite remember, but either way, an important place. He educated us on the ways of granting gratuities to deserving individuals. "Brotha . . . you gotta hit the MAN . . . in the HAND!" he told us in an energetic, almost nursery rhyme like way. He repeated it again and again. "Hit the MAN in the HAND!"

> **TRAVEL TIP:** *Hit the man in the hand in any applicable circumstances.*

We thought about going to New York but we'd only be there for a few hours and being 37 we wanted to sleep rather than go to a bar and possibly end up having too much fun and be hungover for the entirety of the trip.

The next day we woke early and got into our shuttle. Terry had told us that our driver would be "Big Mike." Big Mike was a large black man named Michael. Before any small talk or chatter, I whipped out an American 10 and hit him hard in the hand. Big Mike was ecstatic. He acted like we'd given him $10,000. It was Valentine's Day and he said he'd buy his wife some flowers. He had six kids who were "expensive as hell" and was as sweet a guy as you'd ever meet. He was supposed to drop us off in a designated spot that was on the outskirts of the airport. With me perfectly executing my hit to the hand, he basically carried us onto the plane. Great guy.

On the flight down we watched *Once Upon a Time in Hollywood*. I felt like it prepared us for the trip. I was excited for the prospect of running into Margot Robbie at a dive bar while she was looking for a friendly Canadian couple to show around the city and possibly want to have a threesome with. Kristen's hopes presumably elevated to us having a chance encounter with Leonardo DiCaprio and Brad Pitt in a Hollywood restaurant where they'd ask if she wanted to board their private jet to France and walk the red carpet for some indie film's premier. Either option was good with me.

We arrived early in LA and took a bus and the subway to our hotel.

> **TRAVEL TIP:** *Always take public transportation when you can. It's cheaper and the chances of seeing a four-foot-tall hobgoblin like man singing Iron Maiden with a pet chinchilla on his shoulder are exponentially higher.*

We were staying in East Hollywood, which we found out meant we were basically the only non-Latino people in the area. It also meant that you could wander outside and in 30 seconds or less come across the best burrito you'd ever have.

Luckily, we got to the hotel in time for breakfast. We found out that the buffet had an included "omelette man." I remembered the advice of Terry and hit the omelette man in the hand with a nice crisp $1 bill to hopefully get a few extra green peppers and onions for the week.

> **TRAVEL TIP:** *Always try to find a spot with free breakfast. If you're smart, that one meal can stretch into three—a full day. Get a good seat off to the side where you're hidden but doesn't look like you're trying to hide. Bring a purse*

or backpack and hide it under the seat. Every time you get up to get a coffee, grab something to sneak in the bag. Oranges, apples, bagels, bacon, etc. Make little sandwiches if you can. Wrap it up in a napkin. Take as much as you can carry. If you have a fridge in your room, load it to the gills.

After breakfast, we eventually started walking and wandered into Hollywood. We had a beer at Snow White Cafe and watched the movie of people go by in front of us. It's amazing the moment you finally get to settle in to a place after a day or two of transit. You know that it's your home for the next portion of time and you can sink into everything around you.

A Harlem Globetrotter—or at least a man dressed as one—stood on the street outside the bar spinning a basketball on his finger. For money, he'd put the spinning ball onto *your* finger and let you feel like LeBron James for about 10 seconds before you fell back into your averageness. From the time I was eight till I was 18, I played basketball daily. I can spin a ball on a pencil, an axe, even a toothbrush in my mouth. As the crowd of people gathered around to watch this marvellous and magical act, I walked towards the man and put my finger out. He put the ball on my finger and it began to spin. Everyone clapped. As it spun for a few seconds and reached the point where everyone in the crowd thought, "Well, that sure was a marvellous trick, but now the ball will SURELY fall to the ground since this gangly white man clearly does not have the faculties needed to keep the ball spinning," I bounced the ball off my right knee and caught it directly on my index finger as it continued to spin. The crowd gasped. I swatted the ball with my left hand to speed up the momentum. Cheering began. I bounced it off my knuckles three times in a row as the crowd exploded. "THIS MAN IS A GOD," they thought in unison. I threw the spinning ball back to the Globetrotter man and nodded. He caught it on his finger and nodded back.

After becoming the king of LA. I figured the best way to celebrate was to go to Ripley's Believe it or Not. If not *the* best place in the world, it's clearly in the top three. I watched every episode of the show growing up. The episodes were basically the same. There were three segments with each growing in amazingness as the show progressed. The first part consisted of someone being able to eat something they shouldn't be able to eat: glass, nails, an entire plane, etc. Part two was always about some type of body deformity—think giant nut sac and things like that. The episode would always end with a person hanging from hooks in their skin from a dangerous height. It was a no fail formula.

My favourite episode, and probably some of the best TV ever created, was about a man who tried to kill himself by drinking poison. Fortunately, he didn't die, but the poison basically ate away his stomach and intestines. All he had left in his digestive tract was his now non-functional esophagus. To eat, he had to push food down this tube with his fingers. The whole episode showed this. Every single scene was a detailed visual account of him pushing food down a long tube on the front of his chest. The really exciting thing was that every commercial break emphasized to STAY TUNED FOR AMAZING HOME FOOTAGE. I was hooked. What would this magical secret video possibly show? The amazing home footage ended up being exactly what we'd been seeing all episode, but on a shitty home video camera in the '90s. I've never watched better TV.

When we decided we were going to LA, Kristen was most excited to get to go to Universal Studios. I was most excited about seeing the freak show in Venice. I'd seen hordes of freaks on TV and ones I fortunately stumbled upon in back alleys and stuff like that, but to see a group of them all together would be completely mind-blowing. To see someone over eight feet tall and a man who could lift a giraffe would be a dream come true. I was devastated when I found out that it had shut down. I couldn't understand. I know the world is a little bit more sensitive about things these days, but a freak show is the only opportunity for some of these people. I mean, there's not a lot of great opportunities for Siamese twins in the corporate world. Or George—who made his living eating rusted out bolts from Second World War German tanks— probably isn't going to shine as a barista on Rodeo Drive. Where else are a 1,000-pound ham planet and a bearded woman going to get to travel the world, get paid, and be applauded by thousands every day? Put them all in one spot and let us marvel at their freaky attributes and skills.

With the closing of the Venice Freak Show, Ripley's was the second-best option. In the museum we saw all the amazing things you'd expect: a very large man, a tall man, a skinny man, and they even had some tributes to the hook hangers from the show.

After that we took a stroll on the Walk of Fame. We held hands and looked for two empty stars in a row. That's where our names would be. We later saw a star where a couple's names were engraved together one on top of the other. We didn't know which we preferred. Both options were nice.

We ate at In-N-Out Burger, which I didn't really understand. The fries tasted like cardboard and the burgers were average. It was the busiest place I'd ever seen. I guess it was cheap as dirt though, so I guess it was pretty good.

Day 3

We walked to the Griffith Observatory through fancy neighbourhoods and tried to guess who lived in each house. Saw a presentation on "water" and its importance to life. Apparently it has more purposes than something you consume when you have a hangover. Got great views of the city and the Hollywood sign. Kristen got a migraine so we had to leave early. We went back to the hotel and I rubbed her temples for five hours to try and ease the pain. She went to bed and I got a burrito at El Gran Burrito that made me feel like I went to Mexico. Drank a bottle of wine in the courtyard and listened to my favourite song on repeat.

Day 4

Our four-year anniversary (Plywood anniversary). We went to Beverly Hills and walked Rodeo Drive. Saw a necklace for sale in a window that cost more than Nova Scotia itself. Had Pink's Hot Dogs for lunch. Every celebrity who's ever lived has their picture there. We wanted to get on the wall and thought of saying we were the cute blonde girl and Peter Dinklage from *Game of Thrones* since people told us we both look like them. Thought it may work until we remembered Peter was an actual dwarf and only four feet tall.

After we ate there, we went to The Original Farmer's Market and had a fried chicken burger, pizza, mac and cheese, and doughnuts. Basically, just walked around eating EVERYTHING in the city. We found a sweet dog park where we sat and watched the dogs and people go about. We rated animals. And the people. That night we went to a bar across from our hotel. Where the front door should have been, there was just a weird rubber sheet blowing in the wind. Two guys played pool (a short Latino man, and a guy who looked like Carl Winslow). The place smelled like piss, floor cleaner, and a drug front. We sat at the bar and ordered Pabst Blue Ribbon. Periodically, rough-looking people would come in and give the bartender envelopes of money that she would throw into a safe. I wanted to stay because it felt like a movie, but Kristen said people like us die in those movies so we left after a beer.

Day 5

Did a 22-kilometre hike to the Hollywood sign. It felt like we were standing at the epicentre of something special. I didn't know exactly what, but knew I wanted to be a part of it. Ate Thai food after the hike at a little spot that was so cheap I thought they might actually pay us to eat there. Booked the sauna in our hotel for an hour and smooched in it.

Day 6

Spent the day at Universal Studios. Six thumbs up. Went to Venice that night.

Day 7

We walked from Venice to Santa Monica Pier along the boardwalk. It's an amazing strip vibrating with energy and full of every possible character you could ever imagine. There's skaters, surfers, bodybuilders, buskers, beauties, panhandlers, addicts, vendors, locals, and tourists all blending together in an endless stream of life, possibility and symbiotic unison that lets you know you're fine just the way you are, that your role in all this is to push on doing what you do best: you.

The pier itself was like a little circus. I thought of us living in LA. I'd be a famous musician and Kristen would make art that wowed the masses. I'd record in fancy studios and periodically sneak off incognito to busk on the pier to see if people liked the songs for what they were, not just because I was a celebrity.

We sat on the beach and tried to soak up as much sun as we could into our Canadian February skin. I took pictures of Kristen in her new bikini that was designed with her artwork. I went for a swim but remembered a video I saw of great white sharks off the coast in this exact spot and couldn't relax. Had been averaging 16 kilometres of walking a day. Was nice to relax for a bit.

Day 8:

Hung out on beach again and wrote in a little cafe on the boardwalk. Kristen went to yoga, I ate at Chick-fil-A and got a two-beer-buzz on at a Latino bar. I sat at the bar and talked to the waitress. She'd never heard of Nova Scotia and couldn't believe I wasn't from LA, which made me feel cool.

The man beside me had teardrop tattoos and the outline of something that could kill me under his shirt. I took out a weird little baby blue unicorn covered notebook that in high school you'd get shoved in a locker for, and started to write.

I went to the bathroom and there was ice in the urinal. I'm not 100 per cent sure why, but every once in a while, this is the case in bathroom urinals. I felt bad for Kristen—and all girls I suppose—that they never get the opportunity to go to a urinal with ice in it and try to melt it while peeing. There aren't many things in life more rewarding than that. To see it shrink. To watch it dissipate before your eyes. Pure joy.

That night we sat at the end of Venice Pier. It was a lot different compared to Santa Monica. There were no rides, no restaurants, no anything—just a walkway jutting out into the ocean. It had all the magic that it needed, though. We were deep into the ocean, surrounded by water. We could see the lineup of planes coming to land at the airport. There were hilarious weird birds who had no neck, then a really long neck. Two guys fishing had a radio blasting AC/DC. We talked about the dream trip we wanted to do, "The Big Trip." We'd train across Canada, take the Pacific Coast Highway back to LA, drive Route 66, then fly to Costa Rica for four months. I'd have my second solo album out and Kristen would have her artwork to go along with it. I'd play shows, house concerts, and busk. We'd try to sell as much merchandise as we could to get by. We thought of where we'd go, who we'd meet, and who we'd become along the way. "Thunderstruck" rang through the quiet air as the guys beside us reeled in a fish. We dreamed about what was ahead, inspired by what was around us, which we had found by dreaming earlier.

DARTH VADER'S SLEEP MACHINE

Before I was an artist, I worked as a massage therapist. I also worked as a tree planter, grocery store clerk, dinner theatre actress, retail salesperson, youth programmer and, for half of one shift, a waitress. But that's not really significant. Massage therapy was my calling in many ways. It was active, intimate, therapeutic, and my workplace always smelled like bergamot or lavender. I could work barefoot if I chose and wore elastic-waist pants every day. Most importantly, I met people like Bonnie.

Bonnie was a regular client who would eventually become my mentor and friend. She was a yoga instructor and has a spiritual nature about her that marries logic and reality with softness and acceptance. I always appreciated her honest perspective and that she allowed me, even as *her* massage therapist, to feel comfortable as myself no matter who I happened to be from day to day. Even after I left my career in the healing arts, Bonnie remained a significant woman in my life and would be the instigator for what became one of the most spiritually profound weeks of my life.

In the fall of 2017, Bonnie extended an invitation to a group of yogis in our home community of St. Margaret's Bay to join her for a week of rejuvenation, exploration, and self-love transformation. The week would take place on the south-west coast of Costa Rica the following February. All of the women who said yes to this opportunity were older than I was, and at the time, strangers to me. I was hoping one of my "younger" friends would join the trip. Someone who could relate to my lifestyle and travel pace. Someone who I could stay up late with and find adventure. I would quickly realize that age set no limitations on these women and I was grateful I had them all to myself.

My upcoming week away in CR introduced the conversation of Mike coming along to have an adventure of his own. While I was tucked away in the mountain tops at my vegan, yogi, woo-woo palace, Mike would stay in the thick of Montezuma, where the monkeys howled good morning and the locals quickly learned your name and drink order. He would work on his writing and do his best to ward off the inevitable army of mosquitoes that always seemed to feast on the flesh of his legs and ankles. We would be in the same town, but our experiences would not be alike.

We arrived in Montezuma via plane, shuttle, ferry, and taxi. It's a sleepy beach town that people escape to and realize they never want to leave. Life is a little slower there. The long beaches and Noah's Ark worth of wildlife made for a captivating first impression. The thick nacho chips, drumming in the streets, and laid-back locals made for a memorizing stay. It's a tourist town in many regards, but you somehow feel at one with those who have spent a lifetime in this piece of paradise. The fresh-baked onion bread and cream cheese sold at the market sealed the deal for our love affair with Montezuma. Although we would be apart, Mike and I both felt connected through the jungle-scented air and calls of the seabirds.

Mike would be staying in a private hut atop a small hill. You had to climb about 200 steps to reach the shelter and were almost always greeted by an animal you never knew existed. We just called them "creatures" and so long as they didn't hiss or lunge, we were happy they were there. I would be staying at a place labelled a resort but that felt more like a shared home with all the fixings. Anamaya was like a classy commune. The space was cleaner than my living room when my in-laws came to visit and there were no expectations other than to meet your own needs and desires. Not once did I feel obligation or judgment with either the people or place. Everything else that would happen throughout that week was really just the whip cream on top.

When I first entered Anamaya, there was a young woman checking out from her week-long experience. She looked like a cartoon character that had been drawn to over-exaggerate happiness—a Disney Princess, or someone hired for a dental commercial. She was bright and shiny, full of life. She was smiling. *Really* smiling, with genuine meaning and purpose. I said to the receptionist, "I hope I look like that by the end of the week!"

I was sharing a room with two of the 15 women from Bonnie's tribe. I didn't know either of them, but if first impressions meant anything, I was happy to bunk for the week with these two sweethearts. Sandra and Allison were my roommates with whom I got to share stories of struggle, heartbreak, and perseverance. I thought they were joking when they told me each of them had brought their sleep apnea machines as their permitted carry-on, but turns out once you hit 50, this is a likely travel companion. The machines looked like Darth Vader's helmets when they wore them, but they were surprisingly quiet and ambient. I reflected on the agony of the selection process for *my* carry-on bag and shuttered at the idea of having to replace my journal and snacks with a life support breathing apparatus. It takes a lot of time and strategy to pack the perfect travel bags. Any occupied space should be with something you really need. You're carrying it on your back, after all.

> **TRAVEL TIP:** *Don't waste space with things like hair straighteners and makeup. You won't need them and it's liberating to take a break from this stuff. Machines that make you breathe are okay.*

The "resort" was nothing like big places in many Caribbean destinations. It wasn't a Sandals or Iberostar. It was Central America meets India meets Bali meets any collection of sacred energies and decors designed to elicit tranquility and insight. It was clean, breezy, and elegant in a non-pretentious way. It was just enough to make it feel like home but also an escape. There were big, comfortable daybeds both inside and out, communal tables arranged for our decadent meals, two circular-shaped pools that were kept at a refreshing temperature, and two yoga platforms that enabled even the most uptight yogi to melt into savasana with ease. There were other amenities like a spa, outdoor showers, gift shop, library, and walkable attractions like a butterfly garden and even waterfalls. Not too much, not too little.

Though our Nova Scotia gaggle of gals made up about half of the spots at Anamaya, we were beyond fortunate that each one of our accompanying newfound family members felt as though they too were meant to be there with us. People from all over the world complemented the experience with their presence and smiles. People who, throughout the week, we would connect with and share stories of triumph and hardship alike. We first met each other at opening circle, held on the yoga deck on our first evening. A classic "this is my name; this is where I'm from" but with higher vibrations and widened eyes. Maybe it was our travel brains moving at light speed, or maybe it was the view that throughout the week I made a point to imprint in my mind, but something felt changed in my molecular makeup almost immediately.

There is a special wrinkle on my brain that is dedicated to the view from the yoga deck at this space. Overlooking dozens of trees, plants, flora and fauna, the lush green was the aura around a sunset. There were bird species ranging from vultures to toucans and everything in between. A constant hum of wings and whispers, leaving our senses constantly curious. There were howler monkeys that challenged a dinosaur's roar and a general chorus of insects and wild creatures to keep you on your toes and in the moment. But if you looked beyond all of that magic, there was even more. Rugged coastline, with a family of cliffs, holding hands in a song circle. Mountain peaks that ebbed and flowed in their presence, depending on the mood of the sun. Ocean waves crashing, then napping. It was a painting, a movie, a surreal scene that made living in the moment the only place you wanted to be. It was home for a week, among my new family, under the warmth of the sun and comfort of loving staff. I hoped that Mike was simultaneously feeling the connection to the place. And even more so, to himself.

BEST FRIENDS:
The People You Meet

I sat on the beach alone. I was sad because I was by myself for seven days and didn't have any friends. I couldn't complain, though, being in paradise and all. I knew I'd meet people. And this was the first time I'd ever really got to work solely on writing for an extended period of time. I'd be able to finish my second manuscript. I'd have two novels written and that was exciting.

I leaned up against a fallen palm tree, cracked a cold beer, and looked out at the ocean. The sun set and the darkness rolled in. Soon, a local Costa Rican approached. He made a gesture of snorting cocaine, followed by one of inhaling a joint. As per usual, a drug dealer had found me within 30 minutes. Like all dope pushers in foreign lands, he was a wee little man, scaly and lizard-like. "You like the weed or the coke better Big Guy?" he asked. I don't actually consume either drug, but his question wasn't about that. It was purely about which I preferred. I used to like weed a lot, but now it made me too paranoid. I liked Pablo Escobar's moustache so I guess that kind of made me attached to coke, too. "I suppose weed," I told him.

"I give you good deal . . . very good deal," he said.

I was shocked. This friendly, pleasant, drug dealer sought me out of all the people on the beach and not only started a friendly conversation with me but offered me a discount on his product. I couldn't believe my luck!

"What's your name?" I asked, assuming that we had made it to the name exchange portion of friendship.

"Brandon," he said. I was still in awe over the fact that he was willing to give me a good deal.

"I'm Mike!" I told him and stuck out my hand to shake his. We shook hands and I smiled. It was dark but I can only assume Brandon was smiling too. He sat down and leaned against the log with me.

"Where you from?"

"Canada"

"Oh . . . Toronto!"

"No, we're a little further east, a place called Nova Scotia."

"Oh, Vancouver!"

It was 5,000 kilometres away and the exact opposite side of the country, but Brandon was trying like a good friend would. I couldn't fault him for that.

"Yeah . . . pretty close to there!"

He again asked if I wanted weed. I thought that maybe I'd get a little for Kristen; she could enjoy it after her yoga retreat. I told him that I didn't at the moment, but if I did, I'd find him.

"I give you the good deal Big Guy," he said again.

I had never met anyone so nice. He barely knew me and was willing to go out of his way and give me his product at a discounted rate.

He stood up, so I did too. We pounded fists and I told him to have a good night as he walked off into the darkness. My first friend: Brandon, the drug dealer.

I sat back down by the log and opened another beer. I had a good friend and was feeling pretty optimistic about things. I wondered what adventures myself and Brandon would get into. Maybe I'd invite him back to Canada to visit. He was my best friend and would be forever.

While I dreamed of our future bike rides and sharing full pecan pies that we'd cut directly down the middle and each take a half, two new people came to the log.

"You mind we sit?" a man asked. He was Costa Rican, wore a Slayer shirt and had a short mohawk. He was kind of chubby and looked like he was probably in a gang.

"Oh geez . . . no worries!" I said, inviting them into my space.

The man and a girl sat down across from me. She was cute and tiny with hair to her shoulders and smiled a lot. Their names were Dennis and Ivonne. They were from the outskirts of San Jose and had just arrived in Montezuma for a weekend vacation with friends. They were coming down for a quick beer on the beach and planned to meet up with their friends at an Airbnb for a barbecue.

My initial assessment of Dennis was entirely wrong. While portraying all the characteristics of a tough, slit-your-throat-if-you-looked-at-his-girl-the-wrong-way biker, he was just a big, sweet teddy bear who laughed at everything and was curious about life. Ivonne didn't say much but was really polite and kind. She was shy about her English, even though I could understand her perfectly.

We sat at the log talking and drinking for three hours. They taught me Spanish sayings I forgot immediately, and I told them everything they wanted to know in English. I gave them a beer and now *they* were my new best friends. Dennis was supposed to be barbecuing for his friends but said this moment was too important. I agreed. Ivonne eventually decided to head back to meet up with them. Dennis didn't leave because he was my best friend. He'd be the first one I'd call on Christmas Day to tell him what I got. I'd tell him who I had a crush on but would make him swear secrecy not to tell anyone. And he wouldn't. Because we were that tight.

Brandon was more like my second-best friend now. Still pretty high up but wouldn't necessarily get to sit shot gun when I got my licence.

Life was good in Montezuma. I had a great friend group who had my back through the thick and thin. I told Dennis about a bar I had been to the previous night. We were both kinda shitfaced by this point and decided to go.

We got to the bar and there was a reggae band playing. While my sober opinion of reggae is that every song sounds EXACTLY THE SAME and they only sing about two topics, after a few beach beers with your best bud, it's pretty damn fun. We got drinks and sat down. On the beach I had told Dennis I was a musician. He played drums himself. It was too loud to talk so Dennis just started to air drum along with the music. I figured I better follow suit and whipped out my best air guitar to jam with my pal.

The band on stage was five Costa Rican guys fronted by a dude named Congo who looked exactly like you'd expect a man named Congo singing in a reggae band to look.

Midway through a song, the lead guitar player got up and left, leaving his guitar leaning against a chair. Normally, I wouldn't have done anything, but I was a few sheets to the wind and wanted to impress Dennis. Between songs I asked Congo if I could join in. He just shrugged. I grabbed the guitar and watched the bass player's fingers. The song was simple and I had it figured out in a few seconds. All those reggae songs are just repetitive jams that once you figure out the key, can play along to. I started to get pretty into it, playing solos and noodling on the pentatonic scale. Dennis was going nuts. He stood up cheering and pointing at me. The crowd loved seeing a foreigner who could play along.

I played with the band for about 45 minutes until they took a break. When I went back to sit with Dennis he could barely stand up. He said he had to go to the washroom. A few people came up to give me drinks so I sat there in the glory of free beer, friends, and music.

Dennis came out of washroom and was completely soaked. I'm not sure what he did in there or how he managed to get that wet, but he may as well have stood under the Niagara for 15 minutes.

When he sat down, the first thing he said was: "Let me explain you!"

I had been meditating every day since I had been there, trying to dive deep into my mind to get to the answers of who *I* truly was. I couldn't believe he was going to fill me in on this pivotal detail.

"By all means, Dennis . . . go ahead!"

This had been what I've been searching for my whole life. This is what I've been struggling with, the answer to what makes me *me*.

"I fuck Ivonne, but we do not go out," he said.

It was a fairly interesting take on the essence of "me" but good as anything.

He stood up, dripping water over the bar and said he had to leave. I asked if he knew where he was going and he said, "Don't worry, Dennis!"

He stumbled into the night and I sat in the bar with my free drinks. I smiled, thinking about what I'd write tomorrow.

Vegan Diet

I was at this retreat for many reasons, but it *was* a yoga retreat, and therefore my desire to deepen my practice was certainly an intention. There were two yoga classes a day: one flow class in the morning from 7:30 to 9 a.m. and one candlelight yin class from 6 to 7 p.m. Each class preceded a meal, and though it was optional attendance, we gladly packed the place for every class. We came from various backgrounds and abilities, from yoga instructors to "I've never tried yoga." Each of us enjoyed and benefited from the work equally.

Our yoga instructor Malissa and her assistant April were the most patient, knowledgeable, supportive, magical fairies a group could ask for. I've been practising yoga for many years. This was the best instruction I'd ever received. We challenged and helped each other. We laughed and cried together. We reconnected with yoga as a lifestyle, not just something we do to see how bendy (or *not* bendy) we can be. I saw women in their 70s get up into wheel, crow, and bird of paradise poses. The look of surprise and pride in their eyes was immeasurable. Yoga taught us not only our physical abilities but how opening our minds to the possibility of being capable of something new and challenging was available to us. Pushing these boundaries was at our fingertips and we wanted to touch the unknown. Malissa reminded us to be kind to our bodies but believed we could do a little more. She had us partner up and support one another through these transitions. We were part of it. She was part of it. It was less teacher guides students and more let's do this together as one. All of those happy chemicals were released into our tree and mountain poses. We weren't just holding warrior pose, we were warriors in poses. It was something special.

The evening classes were held on a different platform. Equally beautiful, slightly more intimate. Yin yoga is a slower practice where poses are held for up to five minutes, in effort to release the deeper tissue layers. We used bolsters, straps, blankets, and all things comfy to support our bodies and wrap up our day. Each class was slightly different, but you always left feeling blessed and alive. It was like a calm lullaby, coupled with a sweet forehead kiss. Personally, I find focus and determination with an active flow class and a sense of ease and letting go with a yin practice. It's worth exploring new styles if you're new to yoga and feel there's something special your body needs—it's probably out there.

The food at Anamaya made me feel like I had discovered a new favourite author or genre of music. I had eaten vegan food before, but this was something unearthly. Or rather, entirely earthly.

It's no secret I have a big appetite. I often complain to Mike that I need to lose 10 pounds, usually while slamming a bacon cheeseburger down my throat with more pleasure than a crocodile in a chicken coop. I come from a lineage of women who share this food fetish. I have memories of my grandmother eating a T-bone steak that sagged over the side of her dinner plate like an uncut pie crust. She'd clean that and then suck the bone hoping for that little bit more. I totally do the same when no one is watching. An entire bag of potato chips or eating drippy grilled cheese over the kitchen sink is left for those home-alone nights in my underwear where no one can see how truly savage I can be when it comes to savoury treats. The food experience at Anamaya was equally euphoric to that, except it was prepared by someone with more cooking secrets than Hostess, Ronald McDonald and Ben & Jerry combined.

I didn't know what to expect from an almost exclusively vegan diet. I was vegetarian for a number of years and have dabbled in all sorts of ways of eating in the past but had never been strict vegan. That juicy burger quickly became a distant memory.

We were fed a glorious compilation of fresh, seasonal fruits, warm baked breads with nut butter toppings. We had rainbow salads, yuca shepherd's pies, avocado dressings, plantain nachos, black bean dips, coconut pies, and banana ice creams. We had sugar-free granola, hot local coffee, fresh-squeezed fruit juices, and delicate cucumber and hummus rolls. The food was plentiful, colourful, healthy and fucking delicious. I ate all of it at every meal. We knew the food was authentically local, as we were able to visit the local permaculture farm where everything was produced. The farm supplies ONLY Anamaya Resort and their little restaurant. The growing methods are ones to be learned from. In North America, we practise what is called "comparative advantage" in economic terms. We clear a whack of land and grow one product. Rather than allow species to work and grow symbiotically, nourishing and pollinating each other, we produce enormous amounts of one good and sell it at market price. Financially lucrative, ecologically ridiculous. At the Anamaya farm, you find cocoa cuddled up with banana, next to lemon drop, next to arugula. Visually, an orchestra of nutrient rich bio-intelligence. Seeing and tasting these foods firsthand offered an even higher level of appreciation for what we were putting into our bodies.

I wondered if Mike was still finding the same satisfaction in the onion bread. We managed to communicate via email each day, but knowing he was so handy made me miss him all the more. I invited some of the girl gang down into the now comparably shady suburbs that was "downtown" Montezuma to meet my fella. We gathered at a seaside bar and ordered local ale. We felt like rebels on the loose, the contrast between environments was so great. Mike told me stories about some of the friends he had made and travellers he had met. I told him about my new friend Barbara, who was an entrepreneur in LA. Before I knew the specifics of what she did, I told Barbara I was an entrepreneur too. Turns out she developed sustainable living pods for NASA that would be used for expeditions on Mars. The actual planet.

I make paintings and sell them out of my living room . . . .

We connected nonetheless, though I expect I did more boasting about our new friendship than she did.

Mike told me about his new friends Brandon the drug dealer and Mickey, the hippie who ate his meals by candlelight. I wondered if we would have made these acquaintances if we were travelling together. Married couples are never as approachable as solo travellers. Maybe people feel sorry for us if we're alone and extend companionship out of pity. Maybe people feel that we'd rather be left unbothered when we're together. It's neither good nor bad, just an observation that we've both made. Mostly, we just wanted each other to be safe, happy, and not lonely. Once we both felt satisfied this was the case, our separate roles were resumed. Mike went up one hill and I went up another.

ROUTINES

The night after I met Dennis I stumbled home and couldn't have been happier. I went to the bathroom and, in my drunken bliss, saw a praying mantis walking towards my feet while I sat on the toilet.

A goddamn praying mantis.

I didn't even think. Within a split second, I took the sandal off my foot and crushed it dead on the floor with the bottom of my flip-flop in hand.

I squashed a praying mantis to death while having a shit.

Before then, there were probably 16 to 20 specific shits I'd ever had that I remembered for some reason. After that it was a resounding 17 to 21.

I left the crushed giant there because I didn't feel like cleaning up bug guts at 2 a.m. and figured I'd get a cool picture for Instagram in the morning. When I woke, it was gone. Ants had carried the entire corpse away. Between the lizards, monkeys, bugs, strange pig-like things I see at night in the woods and convince myself aren't actually there, Costa Rica is basically a planet in *Star Wars* with strange, not of this earth creatures.

After that night, I got myself into a good routine. Every day I'd wake up at sunrise to the howler monkeys and their Godzilla cries. Write for four hours. At 10:30 I'd eat breakfast in the common area and see if I could make any new friends. It got to be pretty easy. Mickey was an older guy in his 60s from the islands off Vancouver. He was a gentle soul I could talk to for hours. He lived completely off the grid and made me want to cut my electrical lines and figure out how to grow squash. Emma was in school to be a nurse practitioner and from West Virginia. We talked about dying coal mining towns and the Jonas Brothers. Her ex was best friends with the guys in the band. He'd go away with them for weeks on end while they partied with supermodels and actresses. She was worried he was cashing in on the Jonas Brother lady surplus. I didn't have the heart to say HE ONE HUNDRED PER CENT MOST DEFINITELY IS, so I went with the "he'd sure be an idiot to mess things up with you," which was true because she was super cool. There was George the British bureaucrat, the surfer brothers from Portland, and the Austrian rave girl who turned out to be an orthopedic surgeon.

At noon, I'd go back to the cabin and write for another two hours. In the afternoon, I'd buy a loaf of onion bread, cream cheese, and a fruit bowl. I'd walk along the beach and through the woods till I got to my spot. *My spot* was about a five kilometre jaunt and the most perfect place in the world. It was on the beach, but had palm trees overhead. I could sit in the shade if I wanted or be in the sun. The beach area was only about 20 metres wide and had rocks on either side. Before and after my spot were long, sandy beaches. No one came here. They either stopped before or kept going. I'd sit there, listen to music, meditate and write in my notebook. I'd go for a swim every 20 minutes and sometimes do push-ups or throw rocks around for exercise. There were giant dinosaur birds on the rocks and monkeys would swing through the trees looking for snacks. I'd give them bites of the bread and they'd be my pals. One with a baby on its back came right up to me and I named them Aunt Brenda and Baby Donnie.

After a few hours on the beach, I'd head back and see if any friends wanted to go out to eat. I found a restaurant that was cheap, delicious, and had big portions. I went there every night for supper and ordered the same thing: garlic chicken with rice and veggies. On the fourth night, the owner—Carlos—gave me a big high five and called me "MY FRIEND!" when I walked in. He asked if I wanted the regular and I felt like Neil Armstrong must have when he first took his steps on the moon.

Carlos smoked like a train but you never saw him actually use his hands to smoke. It just hung off his lip like an additional body part.

The first night I went there I asked for a beer. Carlos said they didn't serve beer there, but told me that I could get some across the road at the grocery store and bring it in. I could get cheap delicious food and bring in cheap delicious beer from the outside.

> **TRAVEL TIP***: If it's not cheaper than a can of peas in 1985, don't order drinks with your food. They're expensive and a couple will double the cost of your meal. Order water and pretend you're getting sloshed. Visualize yourself stumbling, slurring words, talking to people out of your league, and you'll get there eventually.*

On night number five, I decided to try something different than my go-to. I had ordered the same meal so many times I could actually say it in Spanish from the menu. *"Filete de pollo al ajillo,"* I'd say and feel like Enrique Iglesias.

That night while I was eating, my good friend Brandon—the drug dealer I met on the beach—came in. I was beyond excited. Seeing a good friend—especially a second-best friend—is always reason to celebrate. I started to smile and looked at Brandon, expecting the same reaction and conversation to ensue. He walked right past me like I didn't exist, like we didn't share a moment together a few nights prior. I couldn't believe it. I was hurt. I thought we had something together. It thought it was real. I had to have been special to get a good deal from him. He couldn't just offer a discount on his drugs to *anyone*! He sat down across from me, leathery and twitchy. Our eyes crossed paths multiple times but he didn't recognize me. I was hurt, but the high five I'd received from Carlos still had me vibrating.

I ordered chicken fajitas instead of my usual garlic chicken. Good, per usual. I thought about taking Kristen there when we were together again. I'd show her how everyone there knew me and loved me. That would sure as hell impress her. "Look," I'd say, "this man, who works 18 hours a day and whose job it is to be kind to customers, has recognized me after repeated visits and transactions. Do you feel even more in love with me?"

"He . . . he . . . just high-fived you!" She'd stutter in amazement.

"We go a long way back."

I'd feel like a king and tell her about the menu. "The garlic chicken is to die for, and the fajitas aren't too bad either."

"What about the . . . ."

"You don't need to worry about anything else . . . ."

I'd pull two beer out of my backpack and she'd be distraught. "What are you doing? You can't take beer into a restaurant!"

"*I* can," I'd say. I'd point to Carlos and give a thumbs up as I drank the beer. Kristen would think I'm the bravest man alive. Carlos would smoke like only he can and give a thumbs up back.

"See?" I'd say.

ᴀNAMAYA GODDESS

art of Anamaya's intention is to consider the body in a holistic matter: mind, body, spirit connection. They offer several opportunities to explore these parts of ourselves and dive deeper into areas that need healing. Their massage and body therapists range in expertise, offering treatments such as shiatsu, reiki, watsu (water massage), reflexology, cranial sacral, tarot reading, and aesthetic services. Our yoga instructor offered a workshop on the "koshas," which everyone raved about. There were also speciality cooking classes, surf lessons, salsa and Spanish classes, and a sunset tour to a local beach. They even offered us a circus performance and proper Latin American feast on our second to last night. Mike and I are usually scouting out the cheapest street food vendor or convenience store crackers on our travels, so this felt like the pinnacle of luxury.

As we had another few weeks of travel ahead of us, we did have to watch our budgets. Rather than buying wine with dinner, I would pick up a bottle at the market and stash it in my room. I didn't invest in many souvenirs (we never do) but chatted with the artisans and learned about their histories. I did, however, indulge in the best massage of my life. I had been harbouring pain on the right side of my body for more than five years. I somehow knew the woman who I booked with was going to help me. The emerald twinkle in her eye gave away all of her loving secrets. She lathered my body in oil, top to bottom, and we just did away with the sheets. She bent me, elbowed me, at one point she climbed on top of me and drove her knees into my kidneys. I laughed and cried and thanked her from the bottom of my heart for giving me the relief I knew I needed. It was the kind of massage you'd lose your licence over in Canada, the kind of massage I had been desperate for. The kind of massage that was treating well beyond my muscles. It's these types of experiences that make me wish our social constructs and regulations were a little more fluid in Canada. You realize how bound we are to norms and expectations when they are so casually explored and broken elsewhere. The willingness to acknowledge what people really need to heal, rather than deprive them for the sake of appropriateness is almost funny to me now. I believe one day we will collectively look back and wonder why the hell we set up our lives to be so voluntarily dysfunctional. For the time being, at least my body was finally functioning better!

I travelled to Anamaya with a group of women I didn't know that well. Aside from Bonnie, I was more or less committed to sharing this vulnerable journey with a group of strangers. When all was said and done, this was easily my favourite part of the week.

As I enter a new age phase in my life, I find myself in a bit of a grey zone. I'm not youthful, I'm not a senior, I'm not retired, and I'm not a mother. I'm in a weird sort of middle-aged era that isn't talked about all that much. I had questions. Having lost both my mother and grandmothers in recent years, I didn't have a resource to inquire about things like menopause and marriage. What's it like to be in your 50s? Or 60s? Or even 70s?

We ranged from age 35 to 75. We had stories of first kisses, of loss, of divorce, and true love. We shared memories of concerts we had seen and dreams fulfilled. We confided in our anxieties, expectations of women in the modern world, how it was exhausting putting others first all the time. We had stories of triumph and defeat, of ambition to make the world more sustainable and beautiful, of our bodies changing and how that was okay. We talked about family, childbirth, adventure, pets, spirituality, and sorrow. We slept when we wanted and ate what we wanted. We were the goddesses of our own worlds and there to support the worlds of our fellow tribeswomen. We were alone and together. We were a sisterhood of all walks of life. We were family.

At the closing ceremony, we were asked to reflect upon our week. What was our favourite part? I emotionally tried to explain what these women meant to me. My mothers and sisters, they had become. My most cherished memory will be the way I was loved and embraced by this community and how they welcomed me as their own.

Anamaya, I left a better version of myself. I left smiling like the very cartoon character I had met on day one.

THE WHALE SHARK

Kristen came back from Anamaya and we shared a perfect day. I introduced her to some friends and took her to my spot on the beach. My monkey pals Aunt Brenda and Baby Donnie came out and we fed them more onion bread. Vultures sat on the rocks and huge dinosaur-like pelicans dove into the water in front of us.

Our time in Montezuma was over. I think we both found what it was we needed. Everything ahead felt right. Everything we wanted in life felt like it was meant to happen on the path we were on.

We packed our backpacks and made our way to the beach where we'd take a boat across the water to a bigger town called Jaco. There were two boats leaving and our position in the lineup put us on the second one. We boarded with a group of about 25 other tourists, all of us a little more tanned and Zen than when we first arrived. There were three Costa Rican men manning the boat, a captain and guys who helped with luggage and whatnot. They made this trip back and forth three times a day for the past 10 years.

The first boat darted away as we took our seats and put on lifejackets. The engine soon started and we were on the move. The coastline of Montezuma got further away as we gained on Jaco in the distance, memories of the small town still fresh in our minds. Without warning, the captain suddenly turned the boat at a sharp angle, almost making a U-turn. A few gasped; I squeezed the deck of the boat with my right hand and grabbed a hold of Kristen with the other. The three Costa Ricans were smiling ear to ear. They started to point into the water. Everyone on the boat turned in unison. In the distance I could see the silhouette of a massive sea creature. The boat stopped. The creature got closer. It was a whale of some sort, its mouth and face incredibly wide. It was silverish blue and covered in white dots. It was a whale shark.

Underneath the body of the massive mammal was another one, a baby. It was tiny and white and swam beside its mom, never more than a few feet away. The mom sparkled in the water, just as curious of us as we were of her. She got closer. I leaned over the side of the boat, my hand sitting atop the water. The giant swam slowly towards us. Something felt monumental about the moment. The water was crystal clear and I could see every detail of the underwater beauty. I dipped my hand into water. Everyone in the boat leaned to one side and I could feel us starting to tilt. It almost looked like she was smiling, like this was just as magical a moment for her. She came to the side of the boat and I leaned down, touching her head for a split second. Immediately after, she sunk back into the water and disappeared with her baby, somewhere into the expanse of the endless Pacific.

I'd assumed that this was something that happened often in these waters. The boat would see a whale shark and stop so the tourists could get a look and snap some pictures for social media. I found out shortly after that the three Costa Rican men had never once in their entire lives seen one. In making the trip three times daily, they'd cross the water six times. In a week that would be 42 trips. In a year that would be 2,184 trips. In 10 years, they crossed that water from Montezuma to Jaco 21,840 times. Not once had they seen a whale shark. Never. What we just experienced was a first for them too. And I could tell. They were just as excited as us. If we had got on that first boat; if we had come to Montezuma sometime in the past 10 years and crossed the water to Jaco on a speed boat any other day and time, this would not have happened.

I held Kristen's hand and we both smiled. We didn't say anything but both knew how special a moment it was. There was nothing that had to be said. We had witnessed something remarkable. I had physically touched the creature, both of us sharing something new together. It felt like the perfect closure to our time in Montezuma. A farewell of discoveries, friendships, firsts but not lasts.

Epilogue: You and Me

Of all the blazing sunsets, mountaintop views, airport sprints, hospitable hosts, spiritual connectivity, joyous new experiences, and creative inspiration, there's one thing we've learned that they all have in common: us. Being lost in a Thai landscape or missing a flight destined for paradise is not only tolerable but becomes part of our grandest stories because we have each other to share them with. Being scared alone is much different than being scared together.

Our sense of adventure is born from the desire to see new things and tackle the unknown. It's about opening our eyes to the world's alternative norms and nuances. It teaches us that our North American cultural beliefs, practices, and traditions are not the only path through life. Travelling has made us more open-minded, culturally aware, and courageous in situations that challenge us. These memories have helped shape our relationship and reminded us that "home" is merely the place we find ourselves together. Whether that's howling with monkeys in Costa Rica, dancing with drag queens in San Francisco, or cozied up by the fire in Nova Scotia, it's our love for each other that promises the journey will be worthwhile.

We've grown to expect, and accept, that while travelling, mishaps are an inevitable part of the adventure. Much like love itself. Committing to the journey and the unexpected twists and turns we are surely to face, is the most anticipated aspect of all. The unknown offers the greatest exhilaration.

In the end, it doesn't really matter where we are. We love our house, but what makes it our home is *us* being in it. It's the *feeling* of home that the two of us create by virtue of occupying a space at the same time.

We take this part of home with us everywhere we go. Togetherness is as familiar as the theme music played on the evening news, the view out our bedroom window, or the smell of our laundry detergent. It's the constant when we're away or at home. Our love is the tool to navigate challenging scenarios abroad and the easy ones at home. Our home is a place of safety, consistency, grounding, and routine. It's the place we take with us.

Being there for each other and helping navigate new lands, injuries, languages, smells, creatures, and currencies makes the destination simply an extension of what home means to us. It's less about the roof under which we sleep and more about knowing that your partner is there underneath it with you. Home can be anywhere. Home is everywhere.

Home is where *You and Me* are together.

Printed in Canada